ARRIVALS AND DEPARTURES

by Alan Ayckbourn

samuelfrench.co.uk

FOR AMATEUR PRODUCTION ENQUIRIES

UNITED KINGDOM AND WORLD
EXCLUDING NORTH AMERICA
plays@samuelfrench.co.uk
020 7255 4302/01

Each title is subject to availability from Samuel French,
depending upon country of performance.

THINKING ABOUT PERFORMING A SHOW?

There are thousands of plays and musicals available to perform from Samuel French right now, and applying for a licence is easier and more affordable than you might think

---

From classic plays to brand new musicals, from monologues to epic dramas, there are shows for everyone.

Plays and musicals are protected by copyright law, so if you want to perform them, the first thing you'll need is a licence. This simple process helps support the playwright by ensuring they get paid for their work and means that you'll have the documents you need to stage the show in public.

Not all our shows are available to perform all the time, so it's important to check and apply for a licence before you start rehearsals or commit to doing the show.

LEARN MORE & FIND THOUSANDS OF SHOWS

Browse our full range of plays and musicals, and find out more about how to license a show
www.samuelfrench.co.uk/perform

Talk to the friendly experts in our Licensing team for advice on choosing a show and help with licensing
plays@samuelfrench.co.uk   020 7387 9373

Acting Editions

BORN TO PERFORM

Playscripts designed from the ground up to work the way you do in rehearsal, performance and study

---

Larger, clearer text for easier reading

Wider margins for notes

Performance features such as character and props lists, sound and lighting cues, and more

---

+ CHOOSE A SIZE AND STYLE TO SUIT YOU

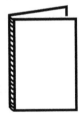

STANDARD EDITION

Our regular paperback book at our regular size

SPIRAL-BOUND EDITION

The same size as the Standard Edition, but with a sturdy, easy-to-fold, easy-to-hold spiral-bound spine

LARGE EDITION

A4 size and spiral bound, with larger text and a blank page for notes opposite every page of text – perfect for technical and directing use

LEARN MORE | **samuelfrench.co.uk/actingeditions**

Mixed Doubles

Mr. A's Amazing Maze Plays

Mr Whatnot

My Very Own Story

My Wonderful Day

Neighbourhood Watch

The Norman Conquests: Table Manners; Living Together;
Round and Round the Garden

Private Fears in Public Places

Relatively Speaking

The Revengers' Comedies

RolePlay

Roundelay

Season's Greetings

Sisterly Feelings

Snake in the Grass

Suburban Strains

Sugar Daddies

Taking Steps

Ten Times Table

Things We Do for Love

This Is Where We Came In

Time and Time Again

Time of My Life

Tons of Money (revised)

Way Upstream

Wildest Dreams

Wolf at the Door

Woman in Mind

A Word from Our Sponsor

**Other plays by ALAN AYCKBOURN
licensed by Samuel French**

The Boy Who Fell Into a Book

Invisible Friends

The Jollies

Orvin – Champion of Champions

Surprises

Whenever

**FIND PERFECT PLAYS TO PERFORM AT
www.samuelfrench.co.uk/perform**

ABOUT THE AUTHOR

Alan Ayckbourn has worked in theatre as a playwright and director for over fifty years, rarely if ever tempted by television or film, which perhaps explains why he continues to be so prolific. To date he has written more than eighty plays, many one act plays and a large amount of work for the younger audience. His work has been translated into over thirty-five languages, is performed on stage and television throughout the world and has won countless awards.

Major successes include: *Relatively Speaking, How the Other Half Loves, Absurd Person Singular, Bedroom Farce, A Chorus of Disapproval,* and *The Norman Conquests.* In recent years, there have been revivals of *Season's Greetings* and *A Small Family Business* at the National Theatre; in the West End *Absent Friends, A Chorus of Disapproval, Relatively Speaking* and *How the Other Half Loves*; and at Chichester Festival Theatre, major revivals of *Way Upstream* in 2015, and *The Norman Conquests* in 2017.

Artistic Director of the Stephen Joseph theatre from 1972–2009, where almost all his plays have been first staged, he continues to direct his latest new work there. He has been inducted into American Theater's Hall of Fame, received the 2010 Critics' Circle Award for Services to the Arts and became the first British playwright to receive both Olivier and Tony Special Lifetime Achievement Awards. He was knighted in 1997 for services to the theatre.

Image credit: Andrew Higgins.

AUTHOR'S NOTE

This play was originally written for an adult cast of eleven actors (six men and five women) plus two non-speaking girls, aged 7–12.

MUSIC USE NOTE

Licensees are solely responsible for obtaining formal written permission from copyright owners to use copyrighted music in the performance of this play and are strongly cautioned to do so. If no such permission is obtained by the licensee, then the licensee must use only original music that the licensee owns and controls. Licensees are solely responsible and liable for all music clearances and shall indemnify the copyright owners of the play(s) and their licensing agent, Samuel French, against any costs, expenses, losses and liabilities arising from the use of music by licensees. Please contact the appropriate music licensing authority in your territory for the rights to any incidental music.

IMPORTANT BILLING AND CREDIT REQUIREMENTS

If you have obtained performance rights to this title, please refer to your licensing agreement for important billing and credit requirements.

ARRIVALS AND DEPARTURES

The World premiere took place on 6 August 2013 at the Stephen Joseph Theatre, Scarborough

With the following cast:

EZ	Elizabeth Boag
QUENTIN	Terence Booth
CHARLES / JESS / HUSBAND	John Branwell
ESME / GIRLFRIEND / DAISY	Rachel Caffrey
MOTHER / HILARY / PAULINE	Sarah Parks
TOURIST / DEBS / DAISY	Emily Pithon
SHERWIN / NORMAN / SON / CERASTES	Ben Porter
STUDENT / FREDDIE / SUSPECT / YOUNG BARRY	James Powell
CHAPLIN / CLIVE / WISBY / ROB	Richard Stacey
NADINE / LILY / WIFE	Sarah Stanley
BARRY	Kim Wall

Director: Alan Ayckbourn
Design: Jan Bee Brown
Lighting: Tigger Johnson
Fight Director: Kate Waters

The New York premiere took place on 29 May 2014 at 59E59 Theaters

With the following cast:

EZ	Elizabeth Boag
QUENTIN	Terence Booth / Bill Champion*

---

* Terence Booth initially played the role of Quentin during the tour, but due to ill-health he had to step down from the role. His part was initially taken by the understudy Peter Halpin before Bill Champion took over for the remainder of the tour and the season at the 59E59 Theaters, New York.

CHARLES / JESS / HUSBAND . . . . Russell Dixon

ESME / GIRLFRIEND / DAISY . . . . Rachel Caffrey

MOTHER / HILARY / PAULINE . . . . .Sarah Parks

TOURIST / DEBS / DAISY . . . . Emily Pithon

SHERWIN / NORMAN / SON / CERASTES. . . . . .Ben Porter

STUDENT / FREDDIE / SUSPECT / YOUNG BARRY. . . . . . . James Powell

CHAPLIN / CLIVE / WISBY / ROB . . . . Richard Stacey

NADINE / LILY / WIFE . . . . Sarah Stanley

BARRY . . . . Kim Wall

Understudy (2014 tour) . . . . Peter Halpin

Understudy (2014 tour) . . . . Lucy McCabe

CHARACTERS

EZ (*formerly* ESMÉ) SWAIN – a soldier, 23

BARRY HAWKINS – a traffic warden, formerly a builder, 50s

CAPTAIN QUENTIN SEXTON (*acting Major*) – O/C SSDO Unit,
aged late 40s

The SSDO Unit

SHANE HUGHES, playing the HUSBAND

CAZ WALTERS, playing the WIFE

DON SIMKINS, playing the SON

RO MERRIVALE, playing the MOTHER

DAVID SCULLION, playing the STUDENT

RITA GILROY, playing the GIRLFRIEND

GRETA TEASDALE, playing the TOURIST

TOMMY WISBY, playing the WORKMAN

The SUSPECT

CERASTES

Ez's Past

NADINE SWAIN – her mother, between 27–37

ESMÉ SWAIN – between 10–12

ESMÉ SWAIN – between 15–18

FREDDIE SWAIN – her father, 28

SHERWIN COOPER – between 32–35

ROB STAGMORE – Esmé's boyfriend between 23–24

CHARLES STAGMORE – Rob's father, 60s

HILARY STAGMORE – Rob's mother, 60s

An ARMY CHAPLAIN

Barry's Past

YOUNG BARRY – between 27–43

DEBS (DEBRA) (NEÉ FOX) – his wife, between 20–35

YOUNG DAISY – his daughter, 7

DAISY HAWKINS – 14

DAISY HAWKINS – 26
JESS FOX – his father-in-law, 55
PAULINE FOX – his mother-in-law, between 50–65
CLIVE WARD – his childhood friend, 30
LILY GILL – Fox's accountant, between 20–41
NORMAN SCULLION – an auditor, 50s

SETTING

A remote area of a London Mainline Rail Terminus and various
half-remembered locations.

TIME

Currently, the present and occasionally the past of Ez's and
Barry's memories.

ACT ONE

A section of a currently disused area of platform at a London mainline rail terminus. Two or three empty benches.

It is early morning with the distant sounds of the station going about its normal business.

Standing alone in the middle of the otherwise deserted area stands QUENTIN, *dark suited, officer in charge of an SSDO (Strategic Simulated Distractional Operations) Unit; whether this group is affiliated to the armed forces, the police force, or to some secret undercover governmental force is never entirely clear. Around his neck is a stopwatch.*

A recently appointed SSDO officer (formerly ETS – Educational Training Squad), QUENTIN *is in his late forties, bespectacled and slightly overweight, probably reaching the end of his desk-bound military career, enthusiastic and determined to make a success of this operation. He is currently addressing his unseen operatives (probably about twenty in all) who seem to be dotted around the platform perimeter.*

QUENTIN *(loudly and authoritatively)* Alright! Listen up, people! We're going to run through it one more time and we're going to keep on running it and running it till we get it absolutely spot on. We've rehearsed this back in the warehouse over the past twenty-four hours and now we're here in situ on the actual station platform where the real thing's due to kick off in just under sixty-six minutes, so we need to be razor sharp. Because I warn you there'll be no second chances. I don't need to remind any of you that this chap, codename Cerastes, is devious, dangerous and deadly as the viper after which he's named. If Cerastes gets the faintest whiff, the slimmest whisker of doubt that this is anything other than totally genuine then, like the reptile he is, he'll slither back into the sand and we'll have lost him again. But this time, that's not going to happen. This time we're going to catch the bastard, this time we're going to nail him before he perpetrates further mayhem on these shores. Our information is good, our tip-off is reliable and this is our best chance of catching him so don't for God's sake let him slip through our fingers again. Let's show the world that SSDO, D group knows where it's at, is totally on top of its onions. Is everyone ready? Businesswoman with briefcase – put the cigarette out, please! At once! Thank you! I've told you about that before, Newton. OK, stand by... on my whistle...starting the whole sequence from the top... *(He blows his whistle and starts his stopwatch)*

QUENTIN *takes his own props from one of the benches, donning a chauffeur's hat to complete his ensemble and holding up a hand-written sign, "GROOMBRIDGE CHEMICALS". He steps to one side, watching critically what ensues.*

The whole ensuing scenarios which now get underway are QUENTIN*'s creations. Some events occur onstage, apparently simultaneously with others out of our sight but to which* QUENTIN *occasionally refers. Offstage, a quartet of football supporters starts to sing drunkenly.* QUENTIN *watches various sequences at once. Including the one visible to us: –*

Sequence 1. A YOUNG HUSBAND *enters carrying a folded baby stroller whilst from the other direction comes the* YOUNG WIFE *holding their baby.*

WIFE Where'd you get to?

HUSBAND Sorry.

WIFE You've been ages.

HUSBAND Sorry. Had to move the car. They wanted me to move the car. *(Starting to unfold the stroller)* You got her to sleep?

WIFE Yes, just a minute ago. Here, hold her a minute, I'll do that. Try not to wake her up again.

The **WIFE** *hands the* **HUSBAND** *the baby while she sees to the bedding in the stroller. The* **HUSBAND** *holds the baby rather casually by its feet, whilst she does this.*

QUENTIN *(seeing this)* Young Husband! You don't hold a baby like that, man. Look at you, you're holding it by its bloody feet, Hughes... Have you never held a baby before?

HUSBAND No, sir, always got away with it so far. Always been lucky, sir...

He unceremoniously hands the baby back to the **WIFE** *who gently places the baby in the chair.*

QUENTIN Well, watch your wife, Hughes! Watch how she holds it. That's good, Walters, that's excellent!

WIFE Thank you, sir. *(Muttering)* Brilliant. Considering I married an idiot.

The couple walk off.

Other sequences continue offstage.

Meanwhile there immediately commences: –

Sequence 2. An anxious **SON** *enters with a bunch of flowers. He stands worriedly waiting for someone. His old* **MOTHER** *eventually arrives pulling her heavy suitcase on wheels with difficulty.* **QUENTIN** *meanwhile has half an eye on other sequences offstage.*

SON *(seeing her)* Mother!

MOTHER *(who sounds younger than she should be)* Hello, Dennis, Son. How are you, boy?

SON *(presenting her with the flowers)* Here! Welcome to London, Mum.

MOTHER Oh, Dennis you shouldn't have...

They embrace.

SON Just a token. *(Indicating her case)* Here, let me take that for you, Mum. *(Lifting the case effortlessly off the ground)* Oh, it's a heavy one, isn't it?

They both move off, her clasping the flowers, him swinging the case.

You haven't lugged this all the way from Hemel Hempstead, have you Mum?

QUENTIN *(glaring at them)* Elderly Mother! Have you got anything at all in that supposedly heavy suitcase, Merrivale?

MOTHER Yes, sir.

QUENTIN What's in there?

MOTHER My lunch, sir.

QUENTIN Your bloody lunch! Well, fill it up with something genuinely heavy. That sort of thing's an absolute giveaway. Completely unconvincing. And when I say heavy, Simkins, I mean heavy. Jump to it, man!

SON Yes, sir.

They both go off.

Sequence 3 immediately gets underway. The student **GIRLFRIEND** *with three paper mugs of hot coffee enters carrying them slowly and carefully. Halfway across, her* **STUDENT** *boyfriend, complete with personal stereo, meets her and takes one of the cups from her. As he does so, he clumsily attempts to kiss her.*

GIRL *(averting her face, irritably)* David, will you stop doing that?

STUDENT You're supposed to be my girlfriend.

GIRL Well, I'm not your sodding girlfriend, don't keep doing that! It's disgusting.

STUDENT (*as they go*) No, but I'm meant to be your boyfriend, aren't I?

GIRL I'm not that desperate...

They go off, presumably to rejoin the rest of their group offstage.

As this sequence finishes: –

Sequence 4 starts. A foreign female **TOURIST** *appears, carrying a heavy rucksack and holding a map. She meets the* **WORKMAN** *coming from the opposite direction, evidently a painter and decorator judging from his splattered overalls.*

TOURIST (*speaking with a slightly dodgy accent*) Excuse, please... excuse...

WORKMAN Yes, darling, what can I do for you?

TOURIST Hig. Hole. Born. Hig Hole Born.

WORKMAN Hig Hole Born? No. Don't you speak any English, darling?

TOURIST No. See. (*Indicating the map*) Hig Hole Born. There. See.

WORKMAN Oh, you mean High Holborn. That's pronounced High Holborn, darling.

TOURIST High Ho Born.

QUENTIN Keep working on that accent, Teasdale! I'm not yet convinced by it!

TOURIST Sir!

QUENTIN Carry on... (*To himself, despairingly*) God!

WORKMAN You're quite a walk from there, darling. Your best bet is go out the main door there and get yourself a taxi.

TOURIST *(as they move to the door)* Taxi? No, I walk, I walk... I walk to High Ho. Need hoss. Tell.

WORKMAN *(as they exit)* Oh, you mean a hostel. Hostel.

TOURIST *(as they exit)* Hostel. Hi Ho Hostel.

They go off. As this and other offstage sequences complete more or less together, QUENTIN *impatiently blows his whistle and stops his watch.*

QUENTIN *(angrily)* Alright, alright, stop stop stop! Hold it right there! That was a dire, disgraceful, disgusting shambles! You ought to be ashamed of yourselves. It's like we never rehearsed it at all. You lot need to get your acts together! We've got – *(Consulting his watch)* – just over forty minutes till the real thing. Football supporters, over there! Yes, you four lurking behind the notice board! I can see you. Have you been drinking? You hear me? Have you been drinking this morning?

CHORUS No, sir.

QUENTIN You sure? Because if I find you've been drinking...

VOICE *(offstage)* We was just acting, sir!

CHORUS *(off, triumphantly)* Yeah! Yeah! Charley Skinner, Oscar winner! Hey! Hey! Hey –!

QUENTIN That's enough of that! You have been warned, you four! Take this seriously or else. Well, we'll just have to keep on doing it, won't we, till we get it right? Back to your start positions, everyone, please!

An offstage groan from the football supporters.

Quickly now! Quickly! The clock is ticking! The clock is ticking, people! And ready? Here we go again!

QUENTIN *blows his whistle and restarts his watch once more, taking up his own position, monitoring things,*

*and occasionally cueing the various sequences to start.
The footballers start up their song again.*

*The sequences re-start as before. Clearly the dialogue
has been largely improvised and starts to vary slightly
from the first take.*

Sequence 1. The young couple enter as before, **HUSBAND**
with the stroller, **WIFE** *with the baby.*

WIFE Where you been?

HUSBAND Had to move the car. They wanted me to move the
car. *(As he starts unfolding the stroller)* You got her to sleep?

WIFE Just this minute. Here, hold her, I'll do that. Try not to
wake her up again.

She hands him the baby while she sees to the stroller. The
HUSBAND *now holds the baby as if handling unstable
nitro-glycerine.*

QUENTIN *(seeing this)* Good! Good! That's a lot better, young
couple with baby. That's better, Hughes.

HUSBAND Thank you, sir...

He hands the baby back to the **WIFE** *who puts the
baby in the chair rather less gently than before. She is
clearly getting bored with the repetition and wedges the
bedclothes round the tot. They move off together.*

WIFE *(as they go, muttering)* How many more times are we
going to do this...

QUENTIN Until you get it right, Walters! Till you get it totally
spot on...

They then walk off together. As they do so: –

Sequence 2 starts the same with the **SON** *standing with
his flowers, though when the old* **MOTHER** *enters she is
now having trouble shifting her suitcase at all.*

SON *(seeing her)* Mother!

MOTHER *(struggling, muttering)* Fucking hell-fire!

SON *(presenting her with the flowers)* Here! Welcome to London, Mum.

MOTHER What you put in here?

SON *(cheerfully)* Breeze blocks.

MOTHER Breeze blocks?

SON *(presenting her with the flowers)* Here you are, Mum, welcome to London.

MOTHER *(hitting him over the head with the flowers)* Stupid pillock!

SON Ow!

QUENTIN That'll do, Merrivale! That's quite enough of that! That's your final warning, you two!

MOTHER Sir!

SON Sir! *(Pulling the case with difficulty)* Oh, Mum, you haven't lugged this all the way from Milton Keynes, have you?

MOTHER Fucking feels like it...

They both exit as before, the SON *lugging off the impossibly heavy case. As this ends: –*

Sequence 3. The GIRLFRIEND *with three paper mugs of hot coffee slowly enters as before. Halfway across she is again met by her* STUDENT *boyfriend who takes one of the cups from her. As she turns away the* STUDENT *touches her bottom. The* GIRL *jumps and spills some of the coffee down her.*

GIRL Oh, shit! David!

The STUDENT *laughs. The* GIRL *turns angrily and throws the contents of one of the mugs down the front of the* STUDENT*'s trousers.*

STUDENT *(reacting)* OW!

QUENTIN Stop that!

STUDENT Ow! That was hot, you know.

QUENTIN *(dangerously)* One more sound...

STUDENT That was hot, sir.

GIRL Cooled you down, anyway...

STUDENT I'm scalded.

The GIRL laughs and goes off.

The STUDENT follows her, unfastening the front of his jeans.

(as he goes) Look at this, she's scalded me.

As this last finishes: Sequence 4. The young foreign female TOURIST carrying a heavy rucksack and holding a map appears, as before. She meets the same WORKMAN coming from the opposite direction.

TOURIST *(in an even dodgier accent)* Excuse, please... excuse...

WORKMAN Yes, darling, what can I do for you?

TOURIST Totty. Cot. Rod. Totty Cot Rod, please.

WORKMAN Sorry, darling, Totty?

TOURIST Totty Cot Rod.

WORKMAN Totty Cot Rod? No. No, never heard of it darling. Sure you're in the right country?

TOURIST No. See. *(Indicating the map)* Totty Cot Rod. There. See.

WORKMAN Oh, Tottenham Court Road. That's pronounced Tottenham Court Road, darling.

TOURIST Totty Court Rod.

QUENTIN *(interrupting)* Just a minute! Teasdale, what the hell sort of accent is that?

TOURIST Norwegian, sir.

QUENTIN Norwegian? Have you ever been to Norway?

TOURIST No, sir.

QUENTIN Well, neither's that woman from the sound of it. The closest she's ever been to Norway is Botswana...

TOURIST I'll try that, then, sir, shall I? Botswanian.

She and the WORKMAN *go off.*

QUENTIN Stop! Stop! That was no better. In fact in some cases it was actually worse. We're against the clock, people, the clock is against us. *(To someone off)* ...Two clergymen over there! You're supposed to be in a hurry...you both look half asleep...get a move on... Carer with man in wheel chair, for God's sake, slow down! It's not a race track, woman, what the hell were you playing at?

VOICE *(offstage)* Running to catch a train, sir!

QUENTIN *(grimly)* Right. We're going to have to go once more...

A chorus of protest from off.

Alright, starting positions again, everyone! On my whistle! Ready?

QUENTIN *has taken up his start position and is poised with watch and whistle ready to restart the proceedings once again, when* EZ *wanders on. She is in her early twenties dressed in a plain dark tracksuit and carrying a rucksack. She appears drawn, tired and rather tense, as if she hasn't slept much of late, altogether low key after the colourful figures that have preceded her.*

(seeing EZ*)* Just a minute! Hold it! You! Who are you? What are you doing here?

EZ *(flat)* I was told to report here.

QUENTIN This is a restricted area. You've no business here. This is off limits to civilians. *(Calling)* Wisby!

EZ *(not fazed by this)* I'm not a civilian. I've been told to report here.

QUENTIN *(calling)* Wisby!

The **WORKMAN** *(*WISBY*) enters.*

WISBY Sir?

QUENTIN Who is this woman? Did you let her through?

WISBY She arrived a few minutes ago, sir. She was standing watching.

QUENTIN Standing watching? This is a top secret operation, man. She had no business watching.

WISBY Thought you knew about her, sir.

QUENTIN She has no business being here. What is she doing here? *(To* EZ*)* What are you doing here?

EZ, who has been standing impassively, now holds out a piece of paper.

What's that? What have you got there? *(Taking the paper from her)* What's this?

He briefly scans the document. The others wait.

(slightly mollified) I see. I see. I've been told nothing about this. I should have been informed about this. Who is this other person? Civilian witness it says? What civilian witness?

EZ *(deadpan)* I'm afraid that's top secret information.

WISBY *smirks secretly.*

QUENTIN *(suspiciously)* I'm going to check this out. I'm going to have it verified. For all I know, you could have forged it. Wait there. Wisby, keep an eye on this woman. Don't let her out of your sight. *(As he sets off, yelling)* Alright, everybody, as you were, stand down! Five minutes! While I deal with this.

QUENTIN *goes off, clutching the document.* EZ *and* WISBY *watch him go.*

WISBY Wanker! *(Slight pause)* No. He's alright. Known worse. *(Sitting on a bench)* Got a ciggie on you, darlin', have you?

EZ *shakes her head. She remains standing.*

What you doing here, then, middle of this circus?

Silence. EZ *does not respond.*

Ah. Top secret, is it?

EZ *does not reply. She appears to be in a world of her own, barely listening to him.* WISBY *seems untroubled by her silence.*

I tell you, don't get mixed up in this unit, darlin'. SSDO. Strategic Simulated Distractional Operations. I volunteered, didn't I? I didn't reckon on running round in circles all day long, play acting, did I...?

His voice fades away as the lights and background sounds change slightly. WISBY's *lips move silently for a second or so longer. Then he freezes, indicating that these memory sections, whatever length they are, in real time occupy only a brief second. This convention is observed throughout the play.*

It is 2000. A different place as we share one of EZ's *memories.*

NADINE, *aged twenty seven, appears holding ten-year-old* LITTLE ESMÉ's *hand. A distant triumphal military band is heard.* NADINE *encourages her young daughter to run and greet someone we cannot see.*

NADINE There's Daddy, Esmé, see. Can you see Daddy, Esmé? Go on, Esmé, say hallo to Daddy. Give Daddy a big hug, Esmé! Run to Daddy, now!

Propelled by her **MOTHER,** **LITTLE ESMÉ** *runs forward, arms outstretched to embrace her father. As she runs off,* **NADINE** *steps back into the shadows and things return to normal.* **EZ***'s fleeting memory has passed. She is smiling to herself rather sadly.* **EZ** *passes a hand in front of her eyes.*

WISBY *(his voice fading back in again)* ...I mean who does he think he is, Shakespeare?

Silence.

Have you read it, then? Shakespeare?

EZ *(without looking at him)* Yes.

WISBY Oh. Intellectual, are you? *(Pause)* You sure you ain't got a smoke on you, darlin'? I'm gasping here. *(Slight pause)* Fuck!

Another silence.

QUENTIN *returns, holding a mobile phone, still clutching* **EZ***'s documentation.*

WISBY *rises.*

QUENTIN Alright, Wisby. I'll take over from here.

WISBY Right sir. *(To* EZ, *without irony, as he goes)* Nice to have chatted with you, Miss.

WISBY *goes.* **QUENTIN** *waits till he's out of earshot.*

QUENTIN *(waving the document)* Alright. I've had this thoroughly checked out and it has been officially ratified. But I'd like it known that I was never informed and I've said to them that your presence here, plus a civilian, is in my view liable to jeopardise this entire operation. I've made that clear. Just keep well away from my people, that's all, well away from them, please.

EZ Certainly will.

QUENTIN *gives her another suspicious look, unable to discern her attitude.* EZ *remains impassive.*

QUENTIN Right, Swain, we haven't got a lot of time. I've been asked to bring you up to speed on this. According to information received, our target, codename Cerastes, parked his hire car at Harrogate station and boarded the 0919 hours, calling at intermediate stations, arriving at Leeds at 0956 hours. There, Cerastes was observed catching the 1015 calling at Wakefield Westgate...

His voice fades away, his lips move for a moment or so, then he freezes. The lights and background sounds have changed as before. We revisit EZ*'s earlier memory in almost exact detail. It is 2000. Band music as before.* NADINE *appears holding* LITTLE ESMÉ*'s hand.*

NADINE There's Daddy, Esmé, see. Can you see Daddy, Esmé? Go on, Esmé, say hallo to Daddy. Give Daddy a big hug, Esmé! Run to Daddy, now!

Propelled by her MOTHER, LITTLE ESMÉ *runs forward, arms outstretched. This time her father,* FREDDIE *aged 28, appears, good-looking and dressed as though returning from a tour of duty. Arms outstretched, he swings his daughter through the air.* NADINE *also runs forward and kisses her* HUSBAND *passionately and tearfully. The three of them move off clinging to each other, a happy family re-united. As they leave, things return to normal and* EZ*'s fleeting memory has passed. She smiles to herself rather sadly.*

QUENTIN *(his voice returning)* ...Doncaster, Grantham, Stevenage – are you listening to this at all, Swain? –

EZ *rubs her eyes again.*

(glaring) – and finally arriving here at 1228 hours. An overall journey time of 3 hours and 9 minutes. Cerastes is apparently still aboard, due to arrive here in just under 40 minutes. Once he steps off that train, my people here will be ready for him, primed and ready to swoop. Once they're mixed in with the hundreds of other people legitimately disembarking from the train, my chaps will be virtually invisible, just another 25 innocent travellers going about their business. Mingling with the throng...

EZ What's to stop him getting off on the way?

QUENTIN Just let him try. We have all intermediate stations covered, with a particularly impenetrable ring of steel round Stevenage.

EZ And you know who you're looking for?

QUENTIN Male, medium height, aged between 25 and 45 wearing a distinctive red and white anorak. That's enough to proceed with.

EZ Unless he takes it off and ditches it. If he knows you're following him, that's the first thing he'll do...

QUENTIN He doesn't know. I can assure you, this operation has been kept tightly under wraps.

EZ Maybe he's chosen to wear a distinctive red and white anorak for that reason? So he'd stand out? Helps him to disappear later.

QUENTIN He has absolutely no idea we're on to him.

EZ *(deadpan)* On the other hand, what if a hundred other blokes get off the train all wearing distinctive red and white anoraks, then?

QUENTIN Oh, don't be absurd –

EZ You never know, maybe they're all the rage in Leeds at the moment, distinctive red and white anoraks –

QUENTIN That will do, Swain –

EZ Maybe they're the latest Yorkshire fashion statement. Eh, lad, I must just go up London in me distinctive red and white anorak, by hecky thump –

QUENTIN *(low and angry)* Listen, I don't care for your attitude, Swain, I can't say I care for it at all. It's coming over as extremely negative and defeatist. I won't countenance that sort of talk, do you hear? Not within earshot of my unit.

EZ Fine by me, mate.

QUENTIN And less of that, Swain. Less of the 'mate', if you don't mind. I note that I do outrank you and I'd be obliged if you'd observe the usual niceties, even within the confines of this covert operation.

EZ I'm so sorry, sir. I didn't realise. I mistook you for a chauffeur.

QUENTIN *glares at her.*

QUENTIN Your witness is here merely to provide additional identification. Belt and braces. When he arrives. Where is he? Why isn't he here, anyway?

EZ He's on his way, sir. He landed ten minutes ago.

QUENTIN Landed? Where?

EZ Battersea.

QUENTIN Battersea?

EZ Heliport. They're currently driving him over from there.

QUENTIN Flying him all the way down from Yorkshire? They must reckon he's worth it. I take it he's worth it, is he?

EZ As worth it as a traffic warden ever gets.

QUENTIN A what?

EZ He apparently tried to write the target a parking ticket.

QUENTIN Oh, dear God. Well as soon as he arrives I'll have him brought over. We'll need to keep a close eye on him.

(As he goes) A Yorkshire traffic warden, that's all we need! Wait there, Swain, don't move!

EZ Sir!

QUENTIN *hurries off. EZ gives his back a rather sarcastic salute. She droops slightly. She is clearly very tired. She sits for the first time on the bench and plunges her head in her hands, massaging her eyes. She stares round the station.*

The lights and sound change.

2002. It is EZ's recollection of a 29 year old NADINE in a patch of sunlight at a military airport with sounds of planes and birdsong faintly heard. She is again accompanied by LITTLE ESMÉ, this time twelve-years-old. Both are dressed sombrely for the ceremonial return of Freddie's body. Solemn music is heard distantly.

An ARMY CHAPLAIN approaches them and exchanges quiet words with them both. Whatever he says proves too much for LITTLE ESMÉ who walks stiffly away from them, shaking her head and struggling to control her tears.

NADINE *(calling after her)* Esmé! Esmé, darling... Don't just walk away... Esmé...!

LITTLE ESMÉ *goes off. NADINE and the CHAPLAIN step back into the shadows and the memory ceases abruptly as QUENTIN returns.*

QUENTIN I've just been glancing over your record, Swain. And I have to say, it makes very sorry reading. Very sorry reading, indeed.

EZ *(muttering)* I thought it was supposed to be confidential.

QUENTIN *(sharply)* What? What did you say?

EZ I thought my record was supposed to be confidential. Sir.

QUENTIN Listen, if I have someone attached to my unit, I need to know their history. Their background. Where they're coming from. I want assurances that they're not going to put the rest of my chaps at risk. Now as far as I can judge, your file comes with a capital T on the front cover.

EZ Trouble?

QUENTIN No, not trouble, Swain, though no doubt there's plenty of that in there too, judging from your attitude. No, the T stands for Tragic. What the hell went wrong, woman? Head of your class, fast track promotion, every prospect of going straight to the top. A proud family tradition. Your father, Freddie Swain, he was a legend in his –

EZ Leave my father out of it, if you don't mind...sir.

QUENTIN Yes, I'd think he'd prefer to be left out of it, too. His daughter drinking, brawling, assaulting her fellow officers...

EZ Is that how they described it?

QUENTIN You put the poor woman in hospital, Swain. You broke her jaw. She's still on sick leave. If your father knew about this he'd die of... *(Realising what he is saying)* ...he'd have... I'm sorry...

EZ Die of shame.

QUENTIN I'm sorry. That was thoughtless.

EZ Except, of course, he's already dead. Like all the best heroes. *(Flatly)* Hooray!

QUENTIN *(not unkindly, moving closer to her)* My God, Esmé, you're a right muddle, aren't you, girl? What on earth went wrong?

EZ *(resenting the familiarity)* Ez.

QUENTIN What?

EZ Ez. I no longer answer to Esmé. Sir. If you don't mind.

QUENTIN *(coolly, stepping back from her)* Very well. If you prefer to take that attitude, in future I'll refer to you as

Private Swain, formerly Second Lieutenant Swain, and, following your pending court martial in a week or so, probably thereafter private citizen Swain. In my opinion the sooner the army gets shot of you the better. You're a disgrace to your...

EZ ...to my non-uniform. Thank you very much, sir.

WISBY *appears.*

WISBY Civilian's arrived, sir. They just delivered him.

QUENTIN Ah, right. Let him through, Wisby, show him through.

WISBY Sir! Bit of a delay. He threw up in the chopper. All over the co-pilot, apparently.

WISBY *goes off briefly.*

QUENTIN This is your traffic warden, presumably. Can I rely on you to keep an eye on him, Swain? Keep him from under our feet.

EZ That's what I'm here for, sir. CBSD.

QUENTIN What?

EZ Civilian Baby Sitting Detail, sir.

QUENTIN Oh, yes. In the unlikely event of trouble, his personal safety is your sole responsibility, is that clear?

EZ I'll take care of him, don't worry.

WISBY *returns with* **BARRY**. *A Yorkshireman in his fifties. He is friendly and eager to be of help, excited by the status of stardom with which he has temporarily been granted.*

WISBY Mr Hawkins, sir.

BARRY *(cheerfully)* How d'y'do?

QUENTIN *(with charm)* Ah, Mr Hawkins, hallo there! Do come
and join us. Quentin Sexton, O/C SSDO, D Division, how
do you do? Thank you so much for agreeing to help us out.

BARRY My pleasure. Entirely my pleasure, squire.

QUENTIN Thank you, Wisby. Carry on.

WISBY Sir!

BARRY Apologise to the bloke for his helicopter, will you? I
left it in a right state.

WISBY *goes off.*

Never want to ride in one of them again. Worse than the big
dipper, eh? We started buzzing sheep over Buckinghamshire.
That's what did for me. All on taxpayer's money, eh? I don't
know. You'll be the man in charge?

QUENTIN *(modestly)* Yes, indeed, I am he.

BARRY What rank are you, then?

QUENTIN Technically, I hold the acting rank of major.

BARRY *(impressed)* Right. Major, eh?

QUENTIN But being an undercover unit, we tend to avoid –

BARRY You'll be my highest so far, then.

QUENTIN Sorry?

BARRY So far today, I've had three sergeants, two corporals,
one lance corporal and a couple of privates. I've also, very
very briefly, had a Captain. Only he was only passing through,
like.

QUENTIN *(a trifle bemused)* Busy day for you, then?

BARRY Not over yet is it? Best is yet to come, eh?

QUENTIN Did you have a pleasant journey down? Apart from
your – er –

BARRY Apart from my incident? Very pleasant, thank you. Speedy. All the way from Harrogate. Well, from a field just outside, actually. Do you know it, at all? Not the field, mind. Harrogate? Do you know it?

QUENTIN No, I can't say I do.

BARRY Oh, it's a grand place. Wonderful folk. You're familiar with Yorkshire, of course?

QUENTIN Only very, very slightly. I'm afraid I'm more of a Dorset man, myself.

BARRY Nature's finest! Nature's finest is Yorkshire!

QUENTIN Yes, so I've heard tell, Mr Hawkins...

BARRY Barry. Call me Barry, please. Everyone calls me Barry.

QUENTIN Barry...

BARRY Except me mother-in-law. She calls me 'im. 'im over there. *(He laughs)*

QUENTIN *(laughing)* Ah, well, mother-in-laws...

BARRY Oh, yes. Too right. You're married then, I take it?

QUENTIN No, no...

BARRY Oh, you should try it. Every man's got to go through it once, eh?

QUENTIN Well, I'll keep dodging, as long as I can.

BARRY Best of luck mate. They'll catch up with you eventually. Women. They always, do. *(To EZ)* Don't you, love? You catch us all eventually. Like the mounties, bless you. Always get your man, don't you, eh?

QUENTIN Oh, er – Mr – Barry, this is – er – this is – Swain. She's going to be – baby – looking after you throughout the – operation.

BARRY Oh, right. How d'y'do, love?

EZ 'llo.

BARRY So you're looking after me, are you - ? Sorry, didn't quite catch your name, love? Suede, was it? What's it they call you? Suede? Like the material?

EZ S-W-A-I-N. Swain.

BARRY Swain? No, that's a new one on me, love. What is it, Welsh?

EZ *(half under her breath)* Jesus!

QUENTIN So, I understand you got a clear sighting of our target, Barry? Of Cerastes?

BARRY Who? Oh, yes him. He was parked illegally, you see. Right on the corner, double yellows, the lot. He should by rights have been towed away...

Lights and sound change, **BARRY***'s lips continue to move but then, as* **EZ***'s new recollection takes flight, both he and* **QUENTIN** *freeze.*

2005. A bus stop. The sound of the bus departing and 15 year old **ESMÉ** *in her school uniform enters, having just jumped off.* **NADINE***, aged 32, stepping out of the shadows, is waiting to meet her.*

ESMÉ *(seeing her* **MOTHER***, embarassed)* Oh, Mum...

She looks round anxiously to see if any of her friends have seen **NADINE***.*

NADINE Hallo, darling.

ESMÉ Mum, you don't have to –

NADINE Have a good day at school?

ESMÉ Yes. Great... You don't have to keep on meeting me like this, you know...

NADINE I know, darling, but –

ESMÉ It's so embarassing. I've told you, I'm alright...

NADINE I was just on my way home from work, darling, and I thought I'd wait for you, that's all...

ESMÉ I'm not going to throw myself under the school bus, am I?

NADINE I know that, darling. You know me. I'm just being silly...

ESMÉ I'm over it, now, I've said. I'm fine now. It was just a passing thing... I'm fifteen, Mum. I'm full of hormones, for God's sake! If I'd really wanted to do it, I'd have chosen a better way than trying to hang myself, wouldn't I –?

NADINE Esmé, you musn't even talk about it –

ESMÉ – I'd have taken Dad's old gun and blown my head off, wouldn't I?

NADINE *(tearfully)* You mustn't say things like that, darling –

ESMÉ Sorry. Sorry...

NADINE I've locked that beastly thing away. Well away! Wretched thing!

ESMÉ I keep telling you there's nothing to – *(Breaking off as she sees someone behind NADINE)* Oh.

SHERWIN, *aged 32, dressed in denim with a pony tail, steps out of the shadows.*

SHERWIN *(smiling)* Hi!

ESMÉ *(staring at him, slightly hostile)* Hi.

NADINE *(nervously)* Esmé, darling, this is Sherwin. Do you remember I told you about Sherwin? From the Arts Centre? He's simply brilliant and he's the guiding light behind everything. *(Linking her arm in his)* Most importantly, he keeps the rest of us in order, don't you, Sher?

SHERWIN *(modestly)* I try my best... Thank God, they're not all as crazy as this mother of yours...

He and NADINE laugh. ESMÉ doesn't.

NADINE I've invited Sherwin to supper with us, Esmé. He forgot to do his weekly shop, poor man. He says there's nothing in his fridge except radishes and spring onions... *(She laughs)*

SHERWIN *(laughing)* Only a single radish, at the last count...

NADINE So I've said he can take pot luck with us. That OK?

ESMÉ *(shrugging)* Whatever you want.

NADINE *(anxious)* Now, only if it's alright with you, darling?

ESMÉ *(walking away)* Nothing to do with me, suit yourselves. Whatever.

SHERWIN *(calling after her, laughing)* If you can bear to put up with a vegetarian for one evening...

ESMÉ *has gone.*

NADINE *(calling after her)* Esmé! Esmé, darling... Don't just walk away... Esmé...! *(Squeezing* SHERWIN*'s arm and smiling)* Sorry. Fifteen year olds, you know...

NADINE *and* SHERWIN *disappear into the shadows as the lights return to normal.*

BARRY *is still telling his story to* QUENTIN, *who is doing his best to appear interested.*

BARRY *(fading up)* ...and I thought to myself, oh, yes, I've got your number, mate. I've got your number. And I had it and all. I had the duplicate there on my pad.

QUENTIN Quite a tale! Which is presumably how they traced him. Via the hire car. And you're positive you'd recognise him again?

BARRY Oh, yes. Certainly. Anyone who's tried to deliberately run you over, you tend to remember. Tweed peak cap. Small dark moustache. Horn rim glasses. Navy blue blazer with brass buttons. Green and blue diagonal striped tie, pale blue striped shirt, grey trousers, grey socks and black lace up shoes, well polished. He was very smartly turned out.

QUENTIN Not a red and white anorak, though?

BARRY Red and white anorak? No. Mind, it was quite mild. May have had one in his boot, possibly.

QUENTIN That's very impressive, Barry. We may need to call upon you again, if necessary...

BARRY That's why I'm here, Major.

QUENTIN ...just in case we need confirmation. Now you must excuse me, time's getting on, and I have one or two things to finalise before we go to red alert.

BARRY Final touches, eh?

QUENTIN Oh, yes.

BARRY Devil's in the detail, as my late father-in-law used to say. Devil's in the detail, Barry...

QUENTIN Very true.

BARRY Never knew what he meant by it, mind, but he made his point.

QUENTIN *(completely lost)* Yes, indeed. Well! See you in a moment or two. You can relax for a bit. Recover from your journey. Half an hour to go yet.

BARRY Stand easy, then? Anything you'd like us to be doing, in the meantime, Major, till the train comes in? Me and Swain here?

QUENTIN I'd advise you to use the time to get acquainted, if I were you. It will help general appearances if you both merged a little.

BARRY Merged? How do you mean, merged?

QUENTIN Try and look familiar. Like – two people travelling together. Father and daughter, perhaps. *(With a glance at* EZ*)* No, sorry, Swain...not... A brother and sist – no. Well, I'll leave you both to dream up a convincing scenario. Excuse me, please.

He blows his whistle. BARRY *and* EZ *watch him.* BARRY *is impressed, she less so.*

(loudly to the squad) Now listen up, people. Unfortunately, we don't have time to go through the whole sequence again –

Some cheering from the direction of the football supporters.

(quietening them) But! But! *(Waiting till there is silence)* But. What I propose to do, is to run through certain sequences individually. And I'm referring to those sequences which I consider are still well below scratch. And I think you know what those sequences are, some of you. I'm going to start with you football supporters who are at present letting the whole unit down –

Some boo-ing from the football supporters.

– and unless they're careful will very shortly find themselves on disciplinary charges! And clergymen in a hurry, don't you two slink away either. I want a word with you, too. Everyone stay at your posts... I'm coming round in person.

QUENTIN *goes off.*

BARRY *(impressed)* Oh, you can tell who's in charge, can't you? Who's the gaffer? Reminds me of the wife in the morning, first thing. *(He laughs)*

EZ *is silent. He is uncomfortable.*

Yes. Yes...

A silence. BARRY *looks round at his surroundings, thoughtful for a moment.*

Father and daughter then, eh? Fancy merging at that, then?

EZ *does not respond.*

No? Well, what else can we be? Husband and wife, perhaps? That's not very likely. Brother and sister? No. Father and daughter, I think it has to be, don't you?

Silence.

I've got a daughter. Daisy. She's a bit older than you is Daisy. She were born on Michaelmas Day. 29th September 1985. That's why we called her Daisy. Michaelmas Daisy, get it? That was Deb's idea. My Wife, Debra. Yes, she's little bit older than you, Swain, is Daisy...

He continues silently, his mouth still moving, as EZ *again remembers. 2006. We are at an airport. 16 year old* ESMÉ *enters. She is in her travelling clothes and carries her small suitcase. She is plugged into her personal stereo, seemingly oblivious to her surroundings.* SHERWIN, *aged 33, hurries on.*

SHERWIN *(seeing her, calling)* Esmé! *(To someone behind him)* She's here, Nadine, I've found her! *(Approaching* ESMÉ*)* Esmé, where did you get to, darling?

ESMÉ *(casually)* Looking round the duty free, that's all.

SHERWIN You might have told us, Esmé. Your mother's been frantic with worry.

ESMÉ I was here, wasn't I?

NADINE, *now aged 33, comes hurrying on.*

NADINE *(slightly tearful)* There you are! Oh, darling where have you been? I was so worried. Wandering off like that... I was so worried about you.

She embraces ESMÉ, *who tolerates the embrace but barely responds.*

So worried, baby!

ESMÉ I was just looking round, Mum. Please don't make such a fuss. You're always making such a drama out of everything.

NADINE This is a busy airport. Full of – all types. You never know who might be – You read such terrible things. You wander off without a word, why shouldn't I get worried? You mustn't keep doing this to us, darling.

ESMÉ OK, put me on a lead, why not, if that's what you want. Woof! Woof!

NADINE Don't be so silly. I'm going to the Ladies' room. Now, stay with Sherwin, please. Promise me. Sherwin, don't let this girl out of your sight! Wait there, both of you!

NADINE *hurries away.*

ESMÉ Talk about a crisis!

SHERWIN Your mother has a point, you know, Esmé.

ESMÉ She's hysterical.

SHERWIN No, she's not.

ESMÉ Burns the toast, she calls the fire brigade. Why doesn't she just calm down for once in her life? Stop panicking for ten minutes...

SHERWIN She's your mother, Esmé. You're all she has in the world. Wait till you're a mother yourself, darling...

ESMÉ *gives a mirthless laugh.*

No, just wait. You'll see... Yes, I know you always hate it when I start getting all paternalistic with you, as you put it...

ESMÉ Yes, I do. Because you're not my father. You never have been, you never will be either.

NADINE *comes hurrying back.*

NADINE *(slightly panicked)* I can't find the Ladies' now! It was over there a minute ago! Where's the Ladies' room gone? They've moved it!

ESMÉ *(pointing, wearily)* Over there, Mum. Just along there. You just walked straight past it.

NADINE Oh, yes. What's it doing over there? Wait there! Both of you!

NADINE *goes off again.*

ESMÉ Duh! Great sign up... LADIES' TOILET. Giant letters. She hasn't even got on the plane yet. *(Mimicking)* "I know we're going to crash! It's in the stars! They say we're going to cra-a-a-sh!"

SHERWIN *(uneasily)* Esmé, please. Don't spoil this holiday as well...

ESMÉ Bet you're glad you came with us now, aren't you?

SHERWIN Your mother needs all the love and support we can give her just at the moment. She's going through a very difficult time.

ESMÉ So, who isn't? Who isn't? Better check she's not flushed herself down the toilet, I suppose. *(She moves off in the direction of* **NADINE,** *mimicking again)* "I'm going to drown..."

SHERWIN *(pleading)* Please, Esmé. Do your best. Do try and have fun, won't you, darling?

ESMÉ *(turning back, with a ghastly leer)* How's this? This look as if I'm having fun, does it?

ESMÉ *goes off.*

SHERWIN Oh, God!

SHERWIN *follows her off, a man with forebodings. The recollection ends. Lights and background sounds return to normal.* **BARRY** *is still talking.*

BARRY How long you been in the army then?

EZ *(suddenly aware of* **BARRY***)* What?

BARRY I said, how long have you been in the army, Swain? How long have you been – like, serving?

EZ Since I was eighteen.

BARRY Eighteen. Right. I've nothing but admiration for the armed forces, you know. I take my hat off to you. Every respect. I mean, I wouldn't do the job you do for all the pubs in Tadcaster...

Silence.

No, you keep our shores secure, don't you? That's the way I look at it. It's a job someone has to do because there's threats out there, aren't there...? Well, you'll know better than me, love. Like this feller we're waiting for. What's he up to, then? Blowing innocent folk up, most like. What sort of person does that? I've never wanted to do that. I've never wanted to blow someone up. I've felt like slapping one or two of 'em occasionally but I've always controlled myself. I've held back. No, it's politics, isn't it? And religion? Me, I can't be doing with either. Get shot of them both, if I had my way. Let decent folk sleep in peace. I mean, have you ever felt like shooting someone? I never have. Have you?

Silence.

No, well I expect it's different for you, being in the army, like. Part of the job, isn't it, in the job description? Shooting people? You, you have to shoot people, occasionally, don't you?

EZ Occasionally.

BARRY Do you mind me asking? Have you ever shot anyone?

EZ *(grimly)* There's always a first time...

BARRY Ah, but only the baddies, eh? Only the baddies. Are you, like, carrying a gun at present, are you Swain?

EZ I've not been officially issued with one.

BARRY Right. That's reassuring, anyroad. Mind, you don't need a gun, do you? Not to look after me, surely?

He laughs. A pause.

I expect you've been trained, though, with firearms. Handling firearms?

EZ *is silent.*

I bet you have. Certificates? Bet you've got your certificates and all, haven't you? Yes. Bet you have. *(Slight pause)* How about unarmed combat, then? I bet you can handle yourself if it came to it, can't you? Bet you know all the moves, don't you? Certificates in that as well, eh? Unarmed combat? Good to have that, isn't it? For a young lass, especially. Streets at night, you know. These days. Always tried to persuade our Daisy to take classes, but...well...

EZ It's not a good thing to rely on. Unarmed combat. Dangerous.

BARRY Dangerous? How do you mean? You're likely to hurt someone, accidentally, like?

EZ You can get overconfident, if you're not careful. There's always someone, people stronger than you. If you're a woman.

BARRY I see. *(Reflecting)* No. I'm not sure I know what you mean, love.

EZ *is silent.*

I don't suppose you're meant to talk about it, are you? Security, eh?

Silence.

Do you mind me asking you how old you are, love? You don't mind me asking, do you?

EZ Twenty three.

BARRY Oh. Right. That'll be five years, then? Five years service? No medals yet, then?

BARRY *waits for* **EZ** *to continue the conversation but she remains silent.*

No. Twenty nine years, me. Twenty nine years of marriage. I should be getting a medal. Twenty nine years of marriage to Debs. That's my wife. Debra. Known as Debs. She deserves one and all. Putting up with me... I tell you...

Silence.

No, I don't see as much of Daisy as I used to. Which is a shame what with her being our only. She lives down this way, these days. With Mark, that's her husband. With their two toddlers. Their twins Andrew and Samantha...

As he continues, the lights change again. 2008. This new recollection is a silent sequence at another station. YOUNG ESMÉ, *now 18, enters with* NADINE, *35, and* SHERWIN, *35, who have both come to see her off.* SHERWIN *is carrying* ESMÉ's *holdall.*

NADINE, *weeping as usual, hugs her daughter emotionally.* ESMÉ *stands stiffly, permitting her* MOTHER *to do this.* SHERWIN *eventually pulls* NADINE *gently away from* ESMÉ *and shakes the* GIRL's *hand rather formally then, by way of an afterthought, gives her a rather ill-timed peck on one cheek.* ESMÉ *steps back a pace, takes her bag from him and walks off down the platform without looking back. The older couple are left waving rather forlornly after her retreating figure. At the sound of* BARRY's *voice, the recollection ends abruptly.*

(his voice cutting across) ...sorry, I must be boring you, Swain. That's me, I'm afraid, I tend to rabbit on sometimes, so I'm told... Bunny merchant! That's what my daughter Daisy used to call me. Bunny merchant. Rabbit, rabbit, rabbit... I was just trying to, you know, merge like he said. Sorry.

EZ Sorry, I was... *(She passes her hand in front of her eyes again)*

BARRY No, just tell me to shut up, if I'm distracting.

EZ Sorry. Stretch my legs.

EZ gets up and moves away from him. **BARRY** *watches her for a second.*

BARRY No, you obviously don't want to merge, do you, lass? Not with me anyway. Not many young women do these days. My merging days are behind me, love. When I was young, would you believe...crawling all over me, they were. One or two, anyway. Well, not exactly crawling, you know. More like wanting to sit next to me, you know...to have lunch or something...

Pause. **EZ** *continues to walk around a little.*

EZ So what made you decide to become a traffic warden? Childhood ambition, was it?

BARRY Oh, no. Not at all. Technically, I'm a Civil Enforcement Officer.

EZ Oh, I see. Impressive.

BARRY Not really. Same job. Different title. Different employer. Like rat catcher – rodent operative, you know. No, I had a late career change. I was a builder originally... Had my own business at one stage. Well, I took it over from my late father in law, it was his originally...

The lights and sound change once more as **BARRY** *continues talking and we are in another of* **EZ**'s *recollections.*

2010. **NADINE,** *aged thirty seven, is waiting at the station. At this point,* **EZ** *herself enters the more recent narrative. Her past and present selves are now the same. Aged twenty, she has just stepped off the train.* **NADINE** *as usual is on the verge of tears. She holds out her arms to embrace her daughter.*

NADINE Darling, welcome home! *(Attempting to embrace* **EZ,** *then remembering)* Oh, no, I forgot, you hate me doing that, don't you?

EZ *(evading the embrace but kissing her briefly on the cheek)* Hallo, Mum. You needn't have bothered meeting me...

NADINE I wanted to, darling. You've been away so long... Ages.

EZ Few weeks, that's all.

NADINE Where's your luggage? Have you lost your luggage?

EZ *(indicating behind her)* No, it's on the trolley over there...

NADINE Don't leave it unattended, darling. Someone will come along and –

EZ Oh, yes? Let 'em try. Did you bring the car? Where's Sherwin? Isn't he with you?

NADINE No. We're no longer together, Sherwin and I. Not any longer. I'm afraid we've split up.

EZ Split up? Why didn't you tell me?

NADINE I didn't want to worry you, darling, while you were doing your – while you were on your manoeuvres –.

EZ For God's sake, Mum, I wasn't on manoeuvres! You could have written and told me, at least. Are you all on your own, then? When did this happen?

NADINE Oh, two or three weeks ago, I can't remember. I cried and cried for days.

EZ I bet.

NADINE I'm over it. It's all behind me now.

EZ What happened?

NADINE I found out he'd been fooling around with Joyce Paite.

EZ Joyce Paite? Who the hell's Joyce Paite?

NADINE One of the art teachers at the Centre. Dreadful faded mousey woman. I only found out because Deirdre let slip she was... I don't want to talk about it here. I've said, it's all behind me. Let's go home, darling. Talk there. And then

I want to hear all your news. Are you pleased to be home, then? You don't have to go back again, do you?

EZ Yes, I have to go back, of course I do. I signed up for ten years, didn't I?

NADINE *(wailing)* Ten years! Oh, my God!

EZ Oh, Mum, please don't start. I told you. Don't start as soon as I get home, please. Now stop it, for God's sake! We're in the middle of the station.

NADINE *(choking back her tears)* You're so cold, Esmé. You don't seem happy to be home at all. Aren't you happy to be home, darling?

EZ Mum, I'm bloody delirious. Now can we go, please? It's freezing on this platform.

NADINE You've always been like this, Esmé. Cold. You've never shown your feelings, have you? You hardly ever cried as a baby, you know?

EZ Mum, you've got enough feelings for both of us. And please don't call me Esmé. I keep telling you, it's Ez now. I'm Ez.

NADINE *(going, with renewed weeping)* Ez! That's so ugly, darling. Esmé's such a pretty name, too...

As NADINE goes, lights and background sounds return to normal. EZ is standing where she was originally, staring with exasperation after her MOTHER. The interruption is this time caused by the swift appearance of QUENTIN, en route from one end of the concourse to another.

QUENTIN *(to himself)* ...hopeless, utterly hopeless. Like talking to a load of neanderthals... *(Irritably, as he passes)* Oh for heaven's sake, try and blend in, you two, will you? Try and merge. Do try and merge...

QUENTIN *goes off again.*

BARRY *(rising guiltily)* Oh, sorry, Major. *(Conspiratorially to EZ)* Oooh. That's us told, eh. That's told us. Well, I suppose we ought to try and do as he says. Try and look like – we're together. Travelling together. Tell you what, I'll come and sit over there by you, shall I? *(He does so)* And then – er – what shall we do to merge? What do you suggest? I know, I'll put an arm round you, just casual, shall I? Like this. I mean, nothing too untoward...

EZ   I'd prefer you didn't do that, please.

BARRY   Sorry?

EZ   I'd prefer you didn't touch me, if you don't mind.

BARRY   *(withdrawing his arm, rather flustered)* Right. Sorry. I mean I didn't mean anything by it, you know. I didn't mean to interfere with your – gun arm or anything...

EZ   Look, you're a nice enough bloke and I've nothing against you personally but we're both here to do a job, right? You're here to observe and hopefully identify a wanted suspect who is probably armed and dangerous. I'm here to look after you and see you come to no harm. That's the extent of my job and the extent of yours. The rest is bullshit. Forget about this merging. Ignore everything that idiot says.

BARRY   Yes, but surely we have to –.

EZ   As soon as the job's over we'll both go our separate ways, never see each other again. I'll go back to my unit and you can go home to Harrogate or wherever you come from and tell your loving wife and daughter and your precious grandchildren all about it and then you can go back to sticking tickets on cars and generally pissing off Yorkshire motorists.

BARRY *is silent. He is rather hurt.*

(realising she went too far) Sorry. It's just we've got nothing in common, have we, not a thing. So why pretend we have, eh?

EZ *sits back on the other seat away from him.*

BARRY *(quietly)* Well, we'll never know now, will we? Whether we have or whether we haven't. We'll never know, will we?

Silence.

If you don't mind me saying, Swain, it sounds as if you've got one or two problems of your own, lass. *(Slight pause)* No, I'll shut up. I won't say another word.

Silence.

Hey! Tell you what, Swain, I've just had an idea! We could pretend we're strangers, couldn't we? Just happened to be sitting here? Yes. That's a good – what did he call it? – a good scenario, isn't it? Hadn't thought of that, had we? Now...

As **BARRY** *sits exploring his new found solution,* **EZ** *takes refuge in another reverie.*

2011. At this point, twenty-one-year-old **EZ** *is seated on her bench when ROB, a fellow trainee officer, aged twenty three, handsome, very top drawer, slides on to the seat beside her. He is holding a couple of plastic bottles of coke, complete with straws.*

ROB *(handing her a cup)* There you go, sunbeam!

EZ Ta.

ROB My treat. Last of the big spenders, me. Don't mind if I sit here, do you?

EZ *(indifferently)* No.

ROB Looked a bit lonely, here. All on your own. Cheers!

They sip their drinks.

Tough old course, eh? I mean, they did warn us at the start that it wasn't going to be a picnic but I was hoping they'd at least throw us an occasional sandwich. I don't know about you but I'm completely knackered. All that good living during the teenage years, I suspect. Coming back to taunt me. No, definitely tougher than I expected. Still, if this is what it takes to become an officer and a gentleman, we'll simply have to grin and bear it, won't we? Correction. Become an officer and a lady, I beg your pardon.

EZ No. Right the first time.

ROB Really? Oh. Oh. I see. *(He stares at her, puzzled)* You're not – you're not one of those by any chance, are you? I mean, I've nothing against them personally, you understand, I just... *(He laughs)* Not that they'd probably let me. Get anything. Up against them personally. *(He laughs)* If you see what I mean... *(Having got in deeper than he intended)* Yeah. Sorry. I didn't mean to...

EZ No, I'm not one of <u>those</u>, as you put it. Nor am I a lady.

ROB I see. How would you classify yourself, then?

EZ I'm a woman. Not a lady. Nor am I a girl. Or a slag. Or a dyke. Or a dolly. Or a bird. Or a bint. I'm a woman. OK?

ROB *(unfazed)* Wow! That narrows it down a bit, anyway. *(Rising and taking her cup)* Finished with that, have you? Well, if you'll excuse me. I must return to the climbing frame. The good sergeant is doubtless itching to make my life a further misery. *(Smiling)* Been nice talking to you – my good woman. *(He bows slightly)*

EZ *stares at him sharply, then smiles, shaking her head.*

Ah! Now when you smile like that, you know, you're beautiful.

EZ What?

ROB *(as he goes)* Beautiful. Drop dead gorgeous. When you smile. More of that, please. More, more, more...

ROB *goes off.*

EZ *stares after him. She smiles to herself. She practices a smile. She catches herself at it. She resumes her customary* *frown. The lights return to normal.* EZ *and* BARRY *are still sitting apart on their separate seats.*

BARRY *has interrupted her recollection by calling across to her.*

BARRY ...off the York train, by any chance?

EZ *(startled)* What?

BARRY I said are you meeting someone off the York train, as well?

EZ *(mystified)* What are you talking about now?

BARRY I'm trying to create the sense of us being strangers. With small talk, like.

EZ *(to herself)* Jesus!

BARRY Are you waiting for the York train, love? Because there's apparently a bit of a wait. Apparently. According to the board back there, there's engineering works at Doncaster. *(Sotto)* That's convincing. There's always engineering works at Doncaster. *(Loudly)* So we may have a bit of a wait, love.

EZ Great.

BARRY Just to warn you.

EZ Thank you.

She shakes her head. A silence.

BARRY Weather's better down here, though, isn't it? Very mild. It were raining in Yorkshire when I left home first thing...

EZ *(groaning)* Oh, God...

BARRY ...you know, for a country as small as ours it's amazing how the weather can vary from place to place. Over quite small areas, too. I mean I could be in West Yorkshire, you know, in blazing sunshine, while in North Yorkshire it'll be pissing down. Amazing. What do they call it? A micro-climate, something like that...?

His voice fades. The lights and background sounds change again.

2012. A railway station. **ROB***, twenty four, is arriving.* **EZ***, twenty two, rises to meet him.*

ROB Hi, darling, thanks for hanging around.

EZ That's OK.

ROB *draws her to him and hugs her. He kisses her lips gently but goes no further.* **EZ***, though she is as relaxed as she possibly can be with* **ROB***, is still stilted in her response.*

ROB Train took forever. I got your text. You get mine OK? Sunday trains, honestly. Spent most of the journey looking at cows, most of which were moving considerably faster than we were. Next time, I promise, I'm driving.

EZ In your car? You're joking. All the way to Bristol?

ROB Eighty thousand miles on the clock, that's all. Plenty of life in the old girl yet. She is but a mere filly.

EZ You won't even make it to Slough.

ROB In which case, I'll persuade them to buy me a new one –

EZ Great. That's always the solution for you, isn't it...?

ROB No, seriously, if Ma and Pa want me to visit, they'll just have to fork out for a new car for me, won't they?

EZ *shakes her head, disapprovingly.*

No, darling, honestly, they can afford it. They're rolling in it. Just sitting there all day in that vast house doing bugger all. Wining and dining with the local gentry, walking those damn great dogs of theirs. Slaughtering the local wild-life... Anyway, great to see you. Missed me?

EZ Yes.

ROB Missed you. Missed you, masses and masses. *(Kissing her face)* Masses and masses of missing. Shame you couldn't come down. We had great fun. How's your mum, anyway?

EZ I think she's alright. She had this new bloke of hers there.

ROB Ah yes, of course the new boyfriend. What's he like?

EZ I think he's more than a boyfriend. Practically moved in with her.

ROB That serious, eh?

EZ Seems to be.

ROB What's he like?

EZ Well – can't really tell. Something odd about him. Not right. Mum's very quiet. For her. Subdued. Which in some ways is no bad thing. But I got the feeling she was...almost... *(She hesitates)*

ROB What? Almost what?

EZ She was almost frightened of him. Just a feeling I got. He was very kind and caring, you know, solicitous. Almost over-doing it. Like it was for my benefit, you know.

ROB Keep an eye on that one, then.

EZ I will.

ROB I'll come with you next time, if you like.

EZ What?

ROB Take a look at him for you. Give him the once over.

EZ No. I'll deal with it. I can deal with it, Rob.

ROB I missed you. All weekend I missed you. Did you miss me?

EZ Yes, I said.

ROB Can't get enough of you, I can't. *(Stroking her bottom fondly)* I'm addicted to you, did you know? And there's no known cure, either.

EZ *(awkwardly)* Rob...

ROB What?

EZ ...come on, not in the middle of the station.

ROB Why not?

EZ People are staring at us.

ROB *(continuing)* Let 'em stare...

EZ *(not enjoying it)* No, please no. Rob, don't... *(Pulling his hands away, irritably)* Don't!

ROB What's wrong? Don't you like me touching you?

EZ I need to be in the mood. You know that.

ROB You're never in the mood...

EZ I'm sorry.

ROB *(angrily)* You're never in the bloody mood are you?

He stamps off rather angrily down the platform, leaving **EZ** *unhappily sitting on the seat.*

EZ *(miserably to herself)* What the hell's wrong with me?

The lights and sounds change and we return to normal. **BARRY** *cuts in again.*

BARRY *(fading up again)* ...it's all to do with the Gulf Stream, of course. I mean but for that, but for the Gulf Stream, you know our climate would be a lot more extreme, apparently. It's to do with the temperature of the water. As opposed to the temperature of the land mass. Fascinating...

EZ Hey! Sorry to interrupt. But how long do you intend keeping this up?

BARRY Sorry?

EZ All this balls about the weather? How long can you keep talking about the weather?

BARRY Well, indefinitely, really. Never gets boring does the weather, eh? Just when you've finished talking about it, it all changes. I tell you, I wouldn't want to live anywhere else but here. Nothing to talk about to strangers, otherwise, is there? No, in my opinion it's one of the things that makes this country great is the weather. *(He laughs)*

EZ *(shaking her head)* You're bloody barmy. *(She smiles one of her rare smiles)*

BARRY Ah! A smile. She's favoured us with a smile. Like the sun's suddenly come out.

EZ *(rising)* Don't raise your hopes, mate.

BARRY Whoops! No it's gone again. Just a little gap in the clouds, there. Progress. We're getting there, though, aren't we? As they used to say on the rail posters. I noticed they soon stopped boasting about that, though, didn't they? *(He laughs)*

BARRY *continues to chatter silently as the lights change again.*

It is 2012. An underground car park. ROB, *24 enters and joins* EZ, *22. He carries both their overnight bags. The atmosphere between them is tense.*

ROB Found a space up on level five. Had to park there. In the open air. Still, I'll shift it later. Cheered up a bit now, have you?

EZ How do you mean?

ROB Three hours in the car and barely a word out of you the whole way from Bristol.

Silence.

Mind you, you've been like that the whole weekend, haven't you?

EZ I haven't.

ROB God, Ez, sitting there through dinner last night with a face like a tombstone. The rest of us brightly trying to make conversation. It's so bloody rude, darling. My parents were wondering what the hell was wrong with you...

Silence.

Can't believe you behaved like that. Felt like putting you over my knee and tanning your bloody backside at one point, I can tell you.

EZ You try it, I'll break your arm.

ROB You would, too, wouldn't you? Given the chance.

Silence between them.

Ez, what the hell's wrong?

Silence.

Not saying, is that it? You just clam up, don't you?

Silence.

One minute everything's fine and suddenly this bloody great black cloud sweeps in from nowhere. What's the matter?

EZ It's just me... It's nothing. Just me...

ROB It wouldn't be so bad if it was just you. Trouble with your black clouds, Ez, you have everyone else reaching for their umbrellas. Come on, out with it. What's the problem? Us? It's got to be us, hasn't it?

Silence. ROB *is about to give up on her when she speaks.*

EZ I just feel everything's moving too fast.

ROB Too fast? How do you mean too fast?

EZ It's all getting too serious, Rob... I need to come up for air.

Pause. He waits.

Whenever we're down there at your parents', it's this assumption that you and I, any minute we're getting engaged and then we'll get married, settle down, have kids. Which means me giving up my career...

ROB Not necessarily. You don't have to give up your career.

EZ What else?

ROB The army are pretty good about that, these days. You can get a quiet job, you know, administrative. A desk job, just for a few –

EZ Great. Thanks very much. If I'd wanted to be a bloody secretary –

ROB You know what I mean...

EZ I'm a professional soldier, Rob. And I want to be one long term. My dad was and I want to be the same. I promised myself I'd do that, ever since the day Mum told me he was... It's just that when we're with your parents... Every time we visit, I can feel it, "Ah-ha, this is the one, the future-daughter-in-law, bearer of our grandchildren –"

ROB Rubbish!

EZ You should hear your mother, Rob, whenever we're on our own. Hilary's practically measuring me up for a sodding wedding shroud. "Are you fond of children, Esmé?" *(Savagely)* Am I fond of them? You bet I am. I eat them as field rations, lady! *(Pause)* I'm sorry, Rob, she's a kind woman. She means well. But she reeks of royal icing and stale confetti. Sorry.

Silence. **ROB** *considers this.*

ROB *(tentatively)* Listen – er – I know you're going to take this the wrong way but – do you think it would help to ease the tensions...your...if we maybe, you know, started sleeping together, do you think? Just a thought. Just an idea...

A silence. **EZ** *is staring at him.*

EZ Have you listened to a single word I've said?

ROB ...no, come on, Ez. Sometimes, it helps to bring you closer. Sex sort of tends to cement a relationship, you know...

EZ *(rising angrily, snatching up her bag)* Jesus!

ROB *(rising too, lamely)* ...gives you both something else in common, you know...

EZ How can we have anything in common, Rob, when you haven't understood a single fucking word I've said?

EZ *storms off.*

ROB *(yelling after her)* Ez! Ez! Don't just walk away, darling! Ez! What the hell's wrong with you?

ROB *kicks his overnight bag in frustration, then gathers it up and goes off the other way as the lights cross-fade to normality.* **BARRY** *is sitting where we left him.* **EZ** *returns.*

BARRY You right, then?

EZ Yes.

BARRY I missed you. You and your cheerful chatter. Still, when you've got to go, you've got to go, eh?

EZ *(smiling faintly)* I do. Specially these days, in my case.

BARRY *(not understanding her)* Oh, right. You missed a bit of excitement, just now...

EZ Oh, yes?

BARRY You know, while you were washing your hands, like, old lady there was struggling with a suitcase. Really heavy, it was. Wor, it were heavy. I tried to give her a hand. Turned out she was, you know, part of your operation. I got a right telling off, from the Major. She was that convincing, she fooled me. Till I got up close to her, like, then I could see she wasn't that old. Wearing a wig, probably. Either that or she'd had some very bad news, lately, eh? *(He laughs)*

EZ smiles, despite herself. BARRY*'s good humour is beginning to get to her.*

Aha! Another smile, that's two! Are we going for the record? Careful, lass, at this rate you'll be having hysterics by the time the train arrives.

EZ *(smiling)* You're barking mad. Are they all like that, where you come from?

BARRY Oh, no. In Yorkshire, I'm regarded as perfectly normal. Bit on the retiring side even...

EZ Remind me to keep clear of that place.

BARRY Why? Frightened it might cheer you up, are you? That you'll have a good time? Go on, lass, you only live once, you know. We pass this way but once, then we're gone. Never to return.

EZ *(dryly)* Oh, that's very deep, that is...

QUENTIN *(approaching, off)* Alright, alright everyone, listen up!

BARRY Hallo, he's back.

QUENTIN *appears.*

QUENTIN Attention, people. Our train is apparently running on time –

BARRY *(winking at EZ)* Miraculously, eh?

EZ smiles again. BARRY *has really got her going and knows he has.*

QUENTIN *(with a sharp look at him)* – and is due to arrive here, re-routed to this platform in precisely five and a half minutes. As far as we know our target, Cerastes, is still aboard. He has not been sighted disembarking at any of the intermediate stations. So we're on course. You will observe that we now have four high visibility police officers positioned at the main exit there, scrutinising every disembarking passenger. In a sense they're acting as our sheepdogs.

BARRY *(softly to* EZ*)* Sheepdogs? Now who's barking mad, eh...

EZ giggles. **QUENTIN** *glares.*

QUENTIN Hopefully, our chap will take note of them and will try and make a detour around this way to avoid them, ducking under the barrier there, which will channel him straight in our direction. That's the plan. The moment that happens, he's so much dead meat.

BARRY Pork pie, preferably... Do with one now, I could.

EZ is now giggling uncontrollably, trying almost agonisingly to contain her laughter and wiping her eyes. **BARRY** *continues to delight in the effect he is having on her.*

QUENTIN Now I cannot emphasise enough that we need to take this chap alive. He's no earthly use to us dead. Alright? So positively no shooting. Clear? Now the second before that train hits the buffers...

BARRY I sincerely hope it doesn't...

EZ continues to giggle.

QUENTIN *(now continuously aware of them)* ...the second before it hits them, on my whistle, let's get this show rolling and on the road! On your toes, overture and beginners, stay sharp and best of luck, people!

BARRY *and* EZ *are both now sharing fits of uncontrollable giggles.*

(glaring at them) What are you two whispering and sniggering about?

EZ Sir.

BARRY Nothing.

QUENTIN Why are you both still sitting on opposite sides? I've said it's not convincing.

BARRY We're strangers.

QUENTIN Strangers?

BARRY We thought it were more convincing, like, if we were to be strangers. We'll be discovered here discussing the weather, we've got it all worked out, haven't we, Swain?

QUENTIN Convincing? Two people sat twenty feet apart, shouting to each other about the weather?

BARRY Oh, you'd be surprised. We'll give him a taster, shall we, Swain? *(Launching into his routine)* Weather's better down here than it was in Yorkshire. It were raining when I left home first thing...

QUENTIN goes off, shaking his head in disbelief.

(continuing unabated) ...for a country the size of ours it's unbelievable how the weather can vary from place to place...

*As **BARRY** continues silently, the lights change again to another station platform. A few weeks ago. **CHARLES** and **HILARY STAGMORE**, a well-to-do couple in their 60s enter. They approach **EZ**, twenty three, solemnly. **EZ** sees them and rises.*

HILARY *(meekly)* Hallo, Esmé.

EZ 'llo.

CHARLES *(grimly)* Esmé.

HILARY We're so, so sorry, to hear about all this, Esmé, we really are. Believe us – the minute we got your letter, we – Charles had a long talk with Robert, hearing his side of it. Didn't you darling?

CHARLES Look, may I suggest before we launch in, that we go somewhere a little more private? This is not something we can discuss in a public place.

EZ Rob's not with you, then?

HILARY No, he – he wasn't – he couldn't...

EZ He didn't think it was worth coming up to London to apologise to me in person?

CHARLES No, he didn't. I advised him that making an apology was virtually an admission of guilt –

HILARY Robert's in a terrible state, terrible.

CHARLES Listen, can we discuss this somewhere quieter, please?

EZ I'm happy enough here. I've nothing to be ashamed of.

CHARLES Well, that's a matter of opinion, too –

HILARY *(cutting in)* Darling! Calmly, please...

CHARLES *(muttering)* We could at least take advantage of the first class lounge...

EZ I thought the whole idea of this meeting was for him to face me in person. Apologise to me in person.

HILARY Esmé, I want you to know that we really do appreciate your decision not to pursue this any further.

EZ I never said that.

HILARY We understood from Robert –

EZ I said I might not pursue it. I never said I wouldn't pursue it.

HILARY It would ruin his life you know that. He has such a wonderful, glowing career ahead of him. Everyone says he has...

EZ Yes, so did I, Mrs Stagmore. So did I.

HILARY Then all because of one moment of stupidity, one evening that started out as a harmless, high-spirited drunken prank turns into this nightmare for everyone concerned –

EZ *(growing angry)* I can't believe you're saying this. Harmless drunken prank? Is that what you're saying –?

HILARY That's what it was, according to Robert.

EZ Drunken, certainly.

CHARLES I understood you'd been drinking, as well?

EZ Yes, I had that night. I admit that. I rarely do but that night I had. What about it?

CHARLES Listen, since we have to discuss this out here. Let's get it over and done with. I've been in the legal profession for the whole of my working life and I can tell you, young lady, that having read your account of what happened and hearing my son's own account, I have to tell you that if you took this to a court of law you wouldn't have a leg to stand on...

EZ laughs.

What is it? What's so funny?

EZ Unfortunate phrase, that's all.

CHARLES It was a drunken party involving the four of you. You were drinking, they were drinking. The truth is now lost in a haze of alcohol. Let's leave it at that. I'm sure there's blame on both sides.

EZ *(quietly)* He raped me, Mr Stagmore. Your son Robert raped me. His two mates pinned me down on the store room floor, watching and laughing, while your son raped me.

CHARLES Robert denies that.

EZ Denies it?

CHARLES He has no memory of that occurring.

EZ Oh, well that's slightly different, isn't it? If he conveniently can't remember –?

CHARLES The others are prepared to back him up –

EZ Then how do they explain that I am now carrying his child?

Silence.

CHARLES Oh, my God.

HILARY How long have you known?

EZ I've suspected it for a few days. I had it confirmed yesterday.

CHARLES We don't know it was Robert. How do we know it wasn't one of the others?

EZ They were both too pissed to try it. I suppose I should consider myself lucky that it was only my fiancé who managed to get it up.

HILARY Listen, Esmé my dear, if there's anything – we can – Please, don't judge Robert too harshly. I know it'll be impossible for you to forgive him completely. But, you must know in your heart he's a good boy. You do, don't you? You mustn't blame him entirely, Esmé.

EZ No, I don't. Nor do I blame those two sad little public school gits that helped him, either. Posh boys having a fun night out, that's all. Having a lark with a little tight-arsed, lower-class bitch with a superglued pussy who wasn't prepared to give it away – yes, right, that's what someone called me the other day, one of my so-called fellow officers. I sorted her out and all – In the end your Robert got bored of waiting, didn't he? So he simply went ahead and took it. But you can't blame him for that, can you? Not entirely. Because that's only how he was brought up, wasn't he? Expecting the world and getting it? Getting things the minute he asks for them? Everything. What's he going to do when someone, who honestly believed he loved her and respected her, goes and says no to him? *(Angrily)* No. No. NO!

A silence. **HILARY** *is shaken.* **CHARLES** *looks grim.*

(quietly) Well, he goes ahead and takes it anyway. By right. I blame you two. That's who I blame, you pair of rich bastards.

CHARLES I'm not listening to any more of this. Excuse me, please. *(He moves away)* Hilary, are you coming?

HILARY *continues to stand there.*

I'll be in the first class lounge.

CHARLES *leaves.*

HILARY Are you – you going to keep the baby or –

EZ I haven't decided yet. There's a little while yet. Before I need to decide. I don't know. I may do.

HILARY If you do decide to keep it, if there's anything we can... *(She trails away)*

EZ *looks at her.*

No. No, of course not. I'm so sorry...

HILARY *hurries away tearfully after her* **HUSBAND**. **EZ** *stands and stares after her. She shakes her head in faint incredulity. The lights return to normal. An approaching train is heard.*

QUENTIN *(offstage)* Alright, everyone! Stand by!

BARRY I say, I say! Swain! I've a feeling things are hotting up.

EZ *(coming back to earth)* Oh. Yes.

BARRY Listen, you can hear the train. Exciting, eh?

EZ Very.

BARRY Hope I'll recognise him again. You know, come to think of it, I'm not sure now whether that moustache and glasses of his were genuine, you know.

QUENTIN *(offstage)* Stand by, everyone!

BARRY Oh, that's it! We're off. Come on, Swain, off we go then.

QUENTIN *enters with his chauffeur's sign, blowing his whistle. Immediately the various sequences get underway simultaneously,* **HUSBAND** *and* **WIFE** *with their baby and stroller routine,* **MOTHER** *and* **SON**, *and* **WORKMAN** *and* **TOURIST**. **BARRY** *and* **EZ** *join in the cacophony with an improvised conversation of their own.*

(launching into their routine) I say excuse me, I don't know you at all, but do you know something? The weather's a lot better down here, than it is up there... Come on, join in, Swain... It were raining in Yorkshire when I left home first thing, this morning. Did you know that?

EZ *(joining in despite herself)* You don't say?

BARRY Amazing, isn't it. You know, for such a small country as ours it's astounding how the weather can change, isn't it?

EZ Mind blowing.

BARRY Over quite small areas, too...

EZ Tiny...

BARRY I mean I can be in West Yorkshire, you know, standing in brilliant sunshine –

EZ Oh, you're from Yorkshire, then?

BARRY How did you guess? Where are you from, lass?

EZ Scotland...

BARRY Scotland? Really? I'd never have guessed that from hearing you...

EZ No, I've been south for a few years. Lost my accent...

BARRY What part of Scotland?

EZ Galashiels.

BARRY Galashiels? Now, remind me again, lass, what part of Scotland is that exactly?

EZ I haven't the faintest bloody idea...

During this the **SUSPECT**, *dressed in a distinctive red and white anorak, enters. He hesitates, seeking a way through the throng.*

QUENTIN *(excitedly)* That's him! Stop him! That's our man!

HUSBAND Here mate, catch!

He throws the baby to the SUSPECT *who involuntarily reaches out and catches it. In the effort of catching it, he trips over his feet, falling flat on his face, clutching the baby like a rugby ball.*

The others members of the team enter from all directions and gather round the SUSPECT, *producing weapons and shouting cacophonously.* EZ *throws herself across* BARRY *protectively pinning him to the bench.*

ALL *(variously)* Keep down! On your face! Don't move! Hands behind your head! Stay there! etc. etc.

QUENTIN *(punching the air triumphantly)* Got him! Got the bastard! Got him! Alright, on your feet, you! On your feet!

The SUSPECT *is handcuffed with a plastic tie and manhandled to his feet by many hands.*

SUSPECT *(in bewilderment)* Bloody hell!

BARRY *(unheard, from beneath* EZ*)* That's not him, you know.

QUENTIN *(not hearing this amidst the hubbub)* Right! Take him into the office there. Just till the van arrives. Take him away.

The SUSPECT *is bundled away by the whole team,* QUENTIN *triumphantly bringing up the rear.*

BARRY I say, excuse me but that's definitely not him.

QUENTIN *(to them both)* Thanks very much, you two. You can both stand down now.

BARRY That certainly wasn't him.

QUENTIN *(ignoring him)* Like clockwork. Not a single shot fired, textbook operation.

EZ Sir!

QUENTIN Yes?

EZ Witness says that wasn't him, sir.

QUENTIN How do you mean, wasn't him?

BARRY I'm saying that wasn't the man. That wasn't the man I had the altercation with.

QUENTIN It wasn't?

BARRY No.

QUENTIN You certain?

BARRY Positive.

QUENTIN I see. *(He reflects)* No, no! Look at his behaviour, that's the behaviour of a guilty man. Running like a scared rabbit. Guilty as hell. Your chap was obviously someone different. That's it. Stand down now. I'll arrange transport to get you back home safely – er – Barry.

QUENTIN *goes out.*

BARRY As long as it's not another helicopter, I couldn't face that again. Well. That's a bit of an anti-climax, isn't it? I'm sure it wasn't the same bloke but I expect they know best, don't they? They're the experts, after all. *(Extending his hand to* EZ*)* It's been good meeting you, Swain. A pleasure spending time with you. I can't say I've got to know you very well, lass, but still. Then again you didn't get to know me very well, either, did you? Another time, eh? Perhaps we'll meet again sometime? Who knows? Probably not, but... Anyroad, I got two smiles out of you, at least, eh? That's something, isn't it?

EZ It's been good to meet you, Barry. You know what? You've gone some way to restoring my faith, mate.

BARRY How do you mean?

EZ My faith in people.

BARRY That's nice. It's nice when that happens, isn't it? *(He smiles)*

EZ *(smiling back)* Yes. Nice.

BARRY Hey! Three! That's the world record. Three smiles! I've done it!

He dances round a little. EZ *stands watching him, smiling.*

(triumphantly) Champion! Yes! Yes! Yes!

QUENTIN *appears in the doorway. They stop.*

QUENTIN As you were. That wasn't him. Wrong man. Wrong man, altogether.

BARRY Ah. *(Slight pause)* Told you so, didn't I?

The lights fade to: -.

Blackout.

End of Act One

ACT TWO

The same.

35 minutes earlier.

Production Note: It is suggested that it could be helpful if sequences repeated from ACT ONE could be physically 'mirror imaged'.

QUENTIN *and* **EZ** *are standing as before.*

WISBY *appears.*

WISBY Civilian's arrived, sir. They just delivered him.

QUENTIN Ah, right. Let him through, Wisby, show him through.

WISBY Sir! Bit of a delay. He threw up in the chopper. All over the co-pilot, apparently.

WISBY *goes off briefly.*

QUENTIN God! Your traffic warden, presumably. Can I rely on you to keep an eye on him, Swain? Keep him from under our feet.

EZ That's what I'm here for, sir.

QUENTIN And in the unlikely event of trouble, his personal safety is your sole responsibility, is that clear?

EZ I'll take care of him, don't worry.

WISBY *returns with* **BARRY**. *A Yorkshireman in his fifties. He is friendly and eager to be of help, excited by the status of stardom with which he has temporarily been granted.*

WISBY Mr Hawkins, sir.

BARRY *(cheerfully)* How d'y'do?

QUENTIN *(with charm)* Ah, Mr Hawkins, hallo there! Do come and join us. Quentin Sexton, O/C SSDO, D Division, how do you do? Thank you so much for agreeing to help us out.

BARRY My pleasure. Entirely my pleasure, squire.

QUENTIN Thank you, Wisby. Carry on.

WISBY Sir!

BARRY Apologise to the bloke for his helicopter, will you? I left it in a right state.

WISBY *goes off.*

Never want to ride in one of them again. Worse than the big dipper, eh? We started buzzing sheep over Buckinghamshire. That's what did for me. All on taxpayer's money, eh? I don't know. You'll be the man in charge?

QUENTIN *(modestly)* Yes, indeed, I am he.

BARRY What rank are you, then?

QUENTIN Technically, I hold the acting rank of major.

BARRY *(impressed)* Right. Major, eh?

QUENTIN But being an undercover unit, we tend to avoid –

BARRY You'll be my highest so far, then.

QUENTIN Sorry?

BARRY So far today, I've had three sergeants, two corporals, one lance corporal and a couple of privates. I've also, very very briefly, had a Captain. Only he was only passing through, like.

QUENTIN *(a trifle bemused)* Busy day for you, then?

BARRY Not over yet is it? Best is yet to come, eh?

QUENTIN Did you have a pleasant journey down? Apart from your – er –

BARRY Apart from my incident? Very pleasant, thank you. Speedy. All the way from Harrogate. Well, from a field just outside, actually. Do you know it, at all? Not the field. Harrogate? Do you know it?

QUENTIN No, I can't say I do.

BARRY Oh, it's a grand place. Wonderful folk. You're familiar with Yorkshire, of course?

QUENTIN Only very, very slightly. I'm afraid I'm more of a Dorset man, myself.

BARRY Nature's finest! Nature's finest is Yorkshire!

QUENTIN Yes, so I've heard tell, Mr Hawkins...

BARRY Barry. Call me Barry, please. Everyone calls me Barry.

QUENTIN Barry...

BARRY Except me mother-in-law. She calls me 'im. 'im over there. *(He laughs)*

QUENTIN *(laughing)* Ah, well, mother-in-laws...

BARRY Oh, yes. Too right. You're married then, I take it?

QUENTIN No, no...

BARRY Oh, you should try it. Every man's got to go through it once, eh?

QUENTIN Well, I'll keep dodging, as long as I can.

BARRY Best of luck mate. They'll catch up with you eventually. Women. They always, do. *(To* EZ*)* Don't you, love? You catch us all eventually. Like the mounties, bless you. Always get your man, don't you, eh?

QUENTIN Oh, er – Mr – Barry, this is – er – this is – Swain. She's going to be – baby – looking after you throughout the – operation.

BARRY Oh, right. How d'y'do, love?

EZ 'llo.

BARRY So you'll be looking after me, will you –? Sorry, didn't quite catch your name, love? Suede, was it? What's it they call you? Suede? Like the material?

EZ S-W-A-I-N. Swain.

BARRY Swain? No, that's a new one on me, love. What is it, Welsh?

EZ *(half under her breath)* Jesus!

QUENTIN So, I understand you got a clear sighting of our target, Barry? Of Cerastes?

During this, EZ retreats into her own thoughts.

BARRY Who? Oh, yes him. He was parked illegally, you see. Right on the corner, double yellows, the lot. He should by rights have been towed away. Anyroad, I was writing his ticket and he come out of this alleyway, just strolling, calm as you like. And he says what you doing and I says I'm ticketing you that's what I'm doing 'cos you're parked illegally and your vehicle in my view constitutes a danger to the public and then I explain to him in detail, smilingly, you know...because I could tell he wasn't local and we're supposed to show good will to visitors so I'm smiling at him, you know, smiling and before I know it, this bloke loses it completely and he snatches the ticket off me pad before I've even had time to bag it and he rips it up and, you know, we're trained to keep calm, it's part of our training, like. And I says, calmly, still smiling, you know, 'cos we're trained, we're encouraged not to get excited and I says, that'll get you nowhere, sunshine, 'cos all I'll do now is write you another one, won't I? And he says, no you effing won't, and he jumps in his car and he tears off, nearly running me over. He would have done, if I hadn't had the sense to jump back, like. And I thought to myself, oh, yes, I've got your number, mate. I've got your number. And I had it and all. I had the duplicate there on my pad.

QUENTIN *(who has been doing his best to appear interested)* Quite a tale! Which is presumably how we traced him via the hire car. You're positive you'd recognise him again?

BARRY Oh, yes. Certainly. Anyone who's tried to deliberately run you over, you tend to remember. Tweed peak cap. Small dark moustache. Horn rim glasses. Navy blue blazer with brass buttons. Green and blue diagonal striped tie, pale blue striped shirt, grey trousers, grey socks and black lace up shoes, well polished. He was very smartly turned out.

QUENTIN Not a red and white anorak, though?

BARRY Red and white anorak? No. Mind, it was quite mild. May have had one in his boot, possibly.

QUENTIN That's very impressive, Barry. We may need to call upon you again, if necessary...

BARRY That's why I'm here, Major.

QUENTIN ...just in case we need confirmation. Now you must excuse me, time's getting on, and I have one or two things to finalise before we go to red alert.

BARRY Final touches, eh?

QUENTIN Oh, yes.

BARRY Devil's in the detail, as my late father-in-law used to say. Devil's in the detail, Barry...

QUENTIN Very true.

BARRY Never knew what he meant by it, mind, but he made his point.

QUENTIN *(completely lost)* Yes, indeed. Well! See you in a moment or two. You can relax for a bit. Recover from your journey. Half an hour to go yet.

BARRY Stand easy, then? Anything you'd like us to be doing, in the meantime, Major, till the train comes in? Me and Swain here?

QUENTIN I'd advise you to use the time to get acquainted, if I were you. It will help general appearances if you both merged a little.

BARRY Merged? How do you mean, merged?

QUENTIN Try and look familiar. Like – two people travelling together. Father and daughter, perhaps. *(With a glance at* EZ*)* No, sorry, Swain...not... A brother and sist – no. Well, I'll leave you both to dream up a convincing scenario. Excuse me, please.

He blows his whistle. BARRY *and* EZ *watch him.* BARRY *is impressed, she less so.*

(loudly to the squad) Now listen up, people. Unfortunately, we don't have time to go through the whole sequence again –

Some cheering from the direction of the football supporters.

(quietening them) But! But! *(Waiting till there is silence)* But. What I propose to do, is to run through certain sequences individually. And I'm referring to those sequences which I consider are still well below scratch. And I think you know what those sequences are, some of you. I'm going to start with you football supporters who are at present letting the whole unit down –

Some boo-ing from the football supporters.

– and unless they're careful will very shortly find themselves on disciplinary charges! And clergymen in a hurry, don't you two slink away either. I want a word with you, too. Everyone stay at your posts... I'm coming round in person.

QUENTIN *goes off.*

BARRY *(impressed)* Oh, you can tell who's in charge, can't you? Who's the gaffer. Reminds me of the wife in the morning, first thing. *(He laughs)*

EZ is silent. He is uncomfortable.

Yes. Yes...

A beat.

EZ is still silent. A pause. BARRY looks round at his surroundings. The lights and background sounds change as we enter, this time round, one of BARRY's recollections. It is 1984 and, spilling on to the platform arrive a small group including YOUNG BARRY, aged twenty seven, and his new bride, DEBS, aged twenty, both off on their honeymoon.

Seeing them off at the station are JESS, fifty five and PAULINE FOX, fifty, his new parents-in-law. Making up the party are his best man, CLIVE WARD, aged thirty, and matron of honour LILY GILL, aged twenty. A great deal of slightly alcoholic merriment.

PAULINE ...and I want a post card from you, every single day, too!

DEBS Every single day? Mum!

CLIVE They're not going to have time for that!

YOUNG B I hope not anyway...

LILY She's not going to get that bored, are you, Debs?

JESS They're on their honeymoon, woman, no time for postcards...

PAULINE You know what I mean...

CLIVE Postcard won't even get here for a month, anyway.

PAULINE I sent my mother one from Ibiza. Every single day of our honeymoon.

JESS I never knew that.

PAULINE Every single day.

JESS Then you must have wrote them lying on your back, that's all I can say!

Ribald merriment all round.

PAULINE That's enough of that, Jess Fox, if you don't mind!

More laughter.

During this **JESS** *draws* **YOUNG BARRY** *to one side away from the others, whose voices fade down proportionately.*

JESS Hey... Hey... *(Confidentially)* Listen, Barry, before you go... *(Producing an envelope from his inside pocket)* ...here. Bit of extra spending money while you're there...

YOUNG B Oh, Mr Fox, no, I can't possibly...

JESS Here, take it. It's all in local currency. You know, Pesetas. I had it converted. I got proper rates. You can't trust the local places... Treat yourselves to a decent dinner. Bit of local jewellery for Debs. Something like that. Whatever you both fancy.

YOUNG B You've been so generous, I mean we've got the house already.

JESS She's my daughter, one and only. I want to see her settled. Listen, Barry, you take care of her, right? She comes to any harm, I'll come round and I'll break your bloody neck, lad.

YOUNG B *(solemnly)* Debs is very precious to me, Mr Fox. I promise, I'll treasure her. I said that in my speech, didn't I? By the way, was it alright? My speech? I mean, I think I went on a bit. Debs told me afterwards, I went on a bit. Once I got going, like, I couldn't stop...

JESS You did her proud, lad. I filled up at one point, I don't mind saying. Now put that in your pocket, before her mother there sees it. Or she'll kill me. Accuse me of spoiling her again.

YOUNG B Well, thank you very much, Mr Fox.

JESS And don't lose it. I know what you're like. Hey, and listen. You're family now. Proper family. You've always been family, but now you're proper family. So no more of the Mr Fox, right. From now on it's Jess, or father-in-law if we're arguing, which I trust we won't be...

YOUNG B Jess, then. I'll try and get used to it. I've been calling you Mr Fox for over 10 years, though, haven't I?

JESS That's another thing, Barry. Soon as you're both back, settled in, I need to talk to you about the business. I've a few more years yet but when I do retire, I'll be looking to you, lad, to take it over...

YOUNG B Me? Oh I don't think I could...

JESS Rubbish!

PAULINE What you two nattering about over there, the train's coming in...

LILY The train's coming in!

CLIVE Typical! Missing his bloody honeymoon, that'll be the next thing...

DEBS Come on, Barry, come on, we'll miss it!

YOUNG B *(hurrying over to them)* Oh, right, I'm coming! I'm coming!

PAULINE Got the tickets safe, have you?

YOUNG B Yes, I got them in... *(Patting his trouser pockets)* Oh, no...where'd I put them? I had them...

DEBS Oh, you haven't lost the tickets now, have you? First the notes for his speech and then the ring and then one of his shoes... I can see I've got a job for life here, haven't I?

YOUNG B *(still searching)* I hope so.

DEBS Where've you put them? If you've lost them, Barry, I swear I'll...

CLIVE Here we are. These the ones?

Handing tickets to YOUNG BARRY.

YOUNG B Oh, that's them!

CLIVE You left them on the dressing table in the spare room.

YOUNG B Oh right. I was changing me trousers, I must have taken them out.

DEBS Oh, thank heavens. Thank you, Clive. *(Kissing him)* A ray of sanity.

LILY Train's leaving! Quickly! He's signalling. The man's signalling. It's leaving!

JESS Come on then, quick, quick, quick...

PAULINE Come on, hurry up. *(Snatching a bag from* DEBS*)* I'll take that...

The wedding party spill off towards the train, grabbing up luggage and bundling the bride and groom before them.

DEBS *(as they go)* God knows if we'll ever make it to Spain...!

As they exit, the lights and sounds return to normal.

BARRY How long you been in the army then?

EZ *(suddenly aware of* BARRY*)* What?

BARRY I said, how long have you been in the army, Swain? How long have you been – like, serving.

EZ Since I was eighteen.

BARRY Eighteen. Right.

Pause.

Father and daughter then, eh? Fancy merging at that, then?

EZ *does not respond.*

No? Well, what else can we be? Husband and wife, perhaps? That's not very likely. Brother and sister? No. Father and daughter, I think it has to be, don't you?

Silence.

I've got a daughter. Daisy. She's a bit older than you is Daisy. She were born on Michaelmas Day. 29th September 1985. That's why we called her Daisy. Michaelmas Daisy, get it? That was Deb's idea. My wife, Debra. Yes, she's little bit older than you, Swain, is Daisy. She'll be – what – oh, well now, she'll be coming up to twenty eight this year, won't she? Can't be twenty eight, can it? Heck, it must be and all. Don't the years just fly by? Fly by? They do when you get to my age, Swain. They fly by...

BARRY *gets lost in his own thoughts again. Lights and background sounds change.*

1992. **YOUNG BARRY**, *aged thirty five, in his overalls is returning from work, carrying his toolbox.* **YOUNG DAISY** *aged seven, dressed for her dance class, hurtles on and grabs her father round the knees in gleeful greeting.* **DEBS**, *aged twenty eight, follows her on.*

YOUNG B *(startled by this sudden attack)* Whooaa! Whoa! Whoa! Hallo, darling...

DEBS *(rather wearily)* **DAISY**, don't do that to Daddy, darling.

YOUNG B She's alright. How's my little Michaelmas, then? How's my Michaelmas Daisy today?

DEBS Daisy, let go, darling. Let go of Daddy.

YOUNG B She's alright, Debs, she's pleased to see me, that's all. Aren't you?

DEBS No, she'll get dirty, won't she? Touching you. You're filthy. Don't touch Daddy, darling, you'll get dirty!

YOUNG B Here you are, then, you carry that in for Daddy, will you, darling? *(Handing her his toolbox)* Put it in the garage for me by the workbench.

YOUNG DAISY *staggers off with the toolbox, clutching it two handed.*

DEBS Barry, those are her dance clothes...

YOUNG B Can you manage, love?

DEBS *(calling after her)* Daisy, be careful! Oh, now she's going to get that all over her... Only just washed that, too. What have you been doing, you're filthy?

YOUNG B Taking a wall down. The old brewery conversion job.

DEBS Thought you were being promoted to a desk job?

YOUNG B I was just helping out. We're one man short this week. I was helping the lads out, you know.

DEBS Dad said he was giving you this desk job.

YOUNG B Well, some of the time. I prefer being outside, though. I don't want to be stuck indoors all day, this weather... I prefer it, really.

DEBS *(moving indoors)* Some of us don't have the choice, do we? Looking after her.

YOUNG B Tell you what, you fancy doing something special tonight?

DEBS *(going off)* I just want to go to bed...

YOUNG B Right. You're on. Bed it is.

DEBS *(sourly)* ...and sleep! I need my sleep, Barry...

They both go off. The lights and sound return to normal.

EZ *is still deep in thought.*

BARRY Do you mind me asking how old you are now, love? You don't mind me asking, do you? I mean, we're supposed to get to know each other, we're meant to merge, aren't we? No disrespect but I seem to be doing most of the merging, aren't I? I sense you're a bit on the private side, you know, keep yourself to yourself and I respect that but...

EZ Twenty three.

BARRY Oh, right. That'll be five years, then? Five years service? No medals yet, then?

BARRY waits for EZ to continue the conversation but she remains silent.

No, twenty nine years, me. Twenty nine years of marriage. I should be getting a medal. Twenty nine years of marriage to Debs. That's my wife. Debra. Known as Debs. She deserves one and all. Putting up with me... I tell you...

Silence.

No, I don't see as much of Daisy as I used to. Which is a shame what with her being our only. She lives down this way, these days. With Mark, that's her husband. With their two toddlers. Their twins Andrew and Samantha.

Pause. EZ appears to be back in her own thoughts again.

No, we don't see as much of them these days. Not as much as we'd like. Still, that's life isn't it? They grow up and they move away. It's only natural. But all the same...

Pause. He realises that EZ is not listening.

Sorry, I must be boring you, Swain. That's me, I'm afraid, I tend to rabbit on sometimes, so I'm told... Bunny merchant! That's what my daughter Daisy used to call me. Bunny merchant. Rabbit, rabbit, rabbit... I was just trying to like, you know, merge like he said. Sorry.

EZ Sorry, I was... *(She passes her hand in front of her eyes again)*

BARRY No, just tell me to shut up, if I'm distracting.

EZ Sorry. Stretch my legs.

EZ gets up and moves away. BARRY watches her for a second.

The lights and background sounds change again.

1999. A railway station. YOUNG BARRY, 42, comes off a train, looking anxious. He is wearing a suit. DEBS, 35, is waiting for him, distraught. YOUNG DAISY, 14, in school uniform, is with her. As soon as she sees her father she runs silently and embraces him, burying her head in his chest. She is clearly distressed. BARRY responds. She continues to cling on to him during the next.

YOUNG B I came as soon as I could, got the first train back. Sorry. Meeting went on for... What happened? How is he?

DEBS It seems he's had a stroke. Mum phoned. He collapsed in the office. They've taken him up to the General. Mum's with him. I've come straight from collecting Daisy...

YOUNG B We'll go straight up there then, shall we? You got the car...?

DEBS No, we can't, Barry. They won't let anyone else in to see him. Only Mum. *(Getting tearful)* She says she doesn't think he even knows where he is. He's lost all his speech and... Daisy, love stop mauling your dad like that, love...

YOUNG B *(stroking DAISY's hair)* She's alright Debs, leave her...

DEBS She's creasing your suit...

YOUNG B She's upset, Debs. She's very close to her grandad...

DEBS So am I. I'm upset, but she doesn't have to worry about your clothes, does she?

YOUNG B *(reluctantly levering* **DAISY** *away)* Yes alright, love. It's alright. First thing is to get you both home, eh? Eh, Daisy? Come on, love, let's get you both home...

Gathering them both up, he guides the sorrowful party to the exit. The lights and sounds change as we return to normal.

EZ is now sitting on the opposite bench.

EZ So what made you decide to become a traffic warden? Childhood ambition, was it?

BARRY Oh, no. Not at all. Technically, I'm a Civil Enforcement Officer.

EZ Oh, I see. Impressive.

BARRY Not really. Same job. Different title. Different employer. Like rat catcher – rodent operative, you know. No, I had a late career change. I was a builder originally... Had my own business at one stage. Well, I took it over from my father in law, it was his originally. I worked for him for eighteen years. Him and his wife, Pauline. She looked after his books, like. Worked for them ever since I were nineteen. Till Jess got poorly and retired, like. Pauline left the firm, too, to take care of him. So I took it over. Ran it for five years. Till the economy, you know, took a turn... No, this current job's still fairly recent. But what do they say? A change is as good as a rest, eh...?

The lights and background sounds change again.

1999. A hospital waiting area. **YOUNG BARRY**, *aged forty two, enters with* **DAISY**, *fourteen.* **DEBS**, *aged thirty five, hurriedly enters from another direction. She stops when she sees them.*

YOUNG B Pauline's still in there with him. They asked us to wait. I expect they're having trouble communicating. She's having problems getting through to him, most like.

He sits on a bench. DAISY *sits by him and rests her head on his lap.* DEBS *sits apart from them.*

DEBS Probably.

YOUNG B *(laughing)* Making it sound like a séance, aren't I?

DEBS What?

YOUNG B Getting through to him? *(In a ghostly voice)* Is there anybody there...? Three knocks for yes... *(He laughs again)*

DAISY *gives a giggle.*

DEBS I'm glad you think it's such a joke, Barry...

YOUNG B No, I was...

DEBS ...it's my father lying in there at death's door, you know...

YOUNG B ...only trying to lighten the atmosphere, Debs. You know.

A silence, while they wait.

DEBS Daisy, don't do that, you're creasing your father's trousers...

YOUNG B She's alright, Debs...

DEBS Just had those dry cleaned...

YOUNG B Leave her... She's alright.

He strokes his daughter's hair. DEBS *looks on disapprovingly. A silence between them.* PAULINE, *aged sixty five, enters, looking grim. The others look at her expectantly.*

DEBS Well?

PAULINE *(shaking her head, grimly)* Well.

DEBS What did he say?

PAULINE He won't be persuaded. He won't listen. I know him when he's like this. Even now when he's... I kept saying to him over and over, are you sure, Jess? You're absolutely certain in your mind? You're sure? And he's nodding away there, determined – thought his head was going to drop off. I kept saying, are you sure you want Barry to take over? And he was set on it.

YOUNG B Well, that's nice, he's determined. He's sure.

PAULINE He's the only one that is... I'm sorry, Barry, but you know my feelings about this. It's too soon for you. You're not ready to step into his shoes. I'm sorry but you're really not... It's too early... *(Noticing* DAISY *for the first time)* Oh, just look at her, there, will you? Isn't that sweet?

DEBS Those are his best trousers...

PAULINE Smart. Still. You know Jess, once he gets an idea... But that's my feeling on the matter. You're too young, Barry.

YOUNG B Well, I'm forty two, aren't I? I'm willing to give it a go. I agree it's earlier than we... I always thought he'd go on for ever, would Jess...

PAULINE He was seventy, three weeks ago, and it's too bloody early to lose him.

DEBS *gives a convulsive sob.*

DAISY We haven't lost him yet, Nan, not yet...

PAULINE We've lost the best of him, Daisy. He'll never be the same again. Never.

A silence. The two women are tearful.

YOUNG B *(brightly)* Well, I'll do my best, if that's what Jess wants. Anyroad, Pauline, I'll have you keeping an eye on things for me, won't I? Keeping me straight.

PAULINE Me? I won't be there to help you. I'll need to stay home nursing Jess, won't I? I can't be doing full time book keeping, not any more.

DEBS Then who –?

PAULINE Lily. It'll have to be young Lily. She'll have to take over. She's been shadowing me long enough. She should be able to cope –

DEBS Lily? Are you sure, Mum? <u>Lily</u>?

PAULINE No, I'm not sure, Debs, I'm not at all sure. *(Going off, distraught)* God help us. God help Fox's with the two of them. Him and her. The blind leading the bloody blind, isn't it? Excuse me, I must catch Debenhams before it closes...

PAULINE goes off hurriedly, blowing her nose. A silence.

DEBS Yes. Well. *(Rising)* Go in and see him, shall we? Put on a brave face, I suppose.

DAISY Mum. Do try and smile, won't you? Try and cheer him up...

DEBS It's all very well for you, Daisy. *(As she goes)* It's all very well for you, love...

DEBS goes off.

YOUNG B Well. You and me can smile for him, Daisy, can't we?

DAISY *(smiling)* Yes, we can smile... *(As they go)* Dad...

YOUNG B What?

DAISY You can do it, you know. You can run the business. Grandad believes you can, I believe you can.

YOUNG B Thank you, Daisy. Thanks very much, love. *(He kisses her lightly)*

As they both go off after DEBS, the lights and sound return to normal.

EZ is still standing.

QUENTIN hurries on, en route from one end of the concourse to another.

QUENTIN *(to himself)* ...hopeless, utterly hopeless. Like talking to a load of neanderthals... *(Irritably, as he passes)* Oh for heaven's sake, try and blend in, you two...do try and merge...

QUENTIN *goes off again.*

BARRY *(rising guiltily)* Oh, sorry, Major. *(Conspiratorially, to* **EZ***)* Oooh. That's us told, eh? That's told us. Well, I suppose we ought to try and do as he says. Try and look like – we're together. Travelling together. Tell you what, I'll come and sit over here by you, shall I? *(He does so)* And then – er – what shall we do to merge? What do you suggest? I know, I'll put an arm round you, just casual, shall I? Like this, I mean, nothing untoward...

EZ I'd prefer you didn't do that, please.

BARRY Sorry?

EZ I'd prefer you didn't touch me, if you don't mind.

BARRY *(withdrawing his arm, rather flustered)* Right. Sorry. I mean I didn't mean anything by it, you know. I didn't mean to interfere with your gun arm or anything...

Pause.

EZ Look, you're a nice enough bloke and I've nothing against you personally but we're both here to do a job, right? You're here to observe and hopefully identify a wanted suspect who is probably armed and dangerous. I'm here to look after you and see you come to no harm. That's the extent of my job and the extent of yours. The rest is bullshit. Forget about this merging. Ignore everything that idiot says.

BARRY Yes, but surely we have to –

EZ As soon as the job's over we'll both go our separate ways, never see each other again. I'll go back to my unit and you can go home to Harrogate or wherever you come from and tell your loving wife and daughter and your precious grandchildren all about it and then you can go back to sticking tickets on cars and generally pissing off Yorkshire motorists.

BARRY *is silent. He is rather hurt.*

(realising she went too far) Sorry. It's just we've got nothing in common, have we. Not a thing. So why pretend we have, eh?

EZ *sits back on the other seat away from him.*

BARRY *(quietly)* Well, we'll never know now, will we? Whether we have or whether we haven't? We'll never know now, will we?

Silence.

If you don't mind me saying, Swain, it sounds as if you've got one or two problems of your own, lass. *(Slight pause)* No, I'll shut up. I won't say another word.

The lights change again to a corridor at **FOX**'s *Builders offices.*

2000. **YOUNG BARRY**, *aged forty three, enters from one direction and* **LILY**, *aged thirty six, smartly dressed for work, enters from another.*

YOUNG B 'morning, Lily.

LILY 'morning, Barry.

YOUNG B Big day, Lily.

LILY Yes. Big day, Barry.

YOUNG B This is where we need to show 'em, eh?

LILY Right.

YOUNG B I've a feeling there's a lot of folk waiting for you and me to fall flat on our faces, make fools of ourselves, eh?

LILY Just one or two...

YOUNG B Well, starting today, we're going to prove 'em wrong, eh, Lily? We're going to get stuck in there and show 'em. Yes?

LILY Yes!

YOUNG B Good luck, then! See you lunchtime. We'll have lunch together, eh?

LILY Lovely.

YOUNG B Just for today, first day. My treat. See you later. *(He makes to leave)*

LILY *(also making to leave)* See you later. *(Stopping)* Barry!

YOUNG B *(stopping)* What?

LILY Good luck to you, too!

YOUNG B Ta.

> **LILY** *goes off to her office.*

> *(to himself)* Think I need that a bit more than you do, lass.

> *As* **YOUNG BARRY** *goes off to his own office, the lights and sound return to normal.*

BARRY Hey! Tell you what, Swain, I've just had an idea! We could pretend we're strangers, couldn't we? Just happened to be sitting here? Yes. That's a good – what did he call it? – a good scenario, isn't it? Hadn't thought of that, had we? Now...

> *He pauses for a second, then calls across to* **EZ,** *who is deep in thought again.*

> Excuse me! Excuse me, I say! Would you be meeting someone off the York train, by any chance?

EZ *(startled)* What?

BARRY I said are you meeting someone off the York train, as well?

EZ *(mystified)* What are you talking about now?

BARRY I'm trying to create the sense of us being strangers. With small talk, like.

EZ *(to herself)* Jesus!

BARRY Are you waiting for the York train, love? Because there's apparently a bit of a wait. Apparently. According to the board back there, there's engineering works at Doncaster. *(Sotto)* That's convincing. There's always engineering works at Doncaster. *(Loudly)* So we may have a bit of a wait, love.

EZ Great.

BARRY Just to warn you.

EZ Thank you.

She shakes her head. A silence.

BARRY Weather's better down here, though, isn't it? Very mild. It were raining in Yorkshire when I left home first thing...

EZ *(groaning)* Oh, God...

BARRY ...you know, for a country as small as ours it's amazing how the weather can vary from place to place. Over quite small areas, too. I mean, I could be in West Yorkshire, you know, in blazing sunshine, while in North Yorkshire it'll be pissing down. Amazing. What do they call it...?

The lights and sound change again.

2005. A motorway service area. Sunshine and distant passing traffic. **BARRY** *himself now enters the more recent narrative, as happened in* **EZ**'s *case. He is currently 48 and is sitting waiting for a meeting with* **NORMAN SCULLION**, *in his 50s, an auditor. They both look rather worried.*

NORMAN *(as he enters)* ...sorry for all this cloak and dagger stuff, Barry. I don't mean to seem dramatic but the walls in that Fox's building are pretty thin and I didn't want to discuss this, not there...

BARRY Right. What's the problem, Norman? Secret meetings in a motorway sevice station. Makes me feel a bit like a drug dealer. It must be quite serious, dragging me out here... I mean, I know business has been a bit disappointing, of late. There's been a general down-turn of course and then we've lost one or two big orders which was a bit disappointing but we're hoping to make them up in the course of time but –

NORMAN It's far more serious than that, Barry. It really is.

BARRY More serious? How do you mean?

NORMAN Yes, true, your income's down, there's no denying that. Considerably down on what it was five years ago. But, as you say, income is something you can tackle, long term. Hopefully. No, the real problem's your outgoings. The past few months they're through the roof.

BARRY Outgoings? How the hell's that happened? We've been scrupulous, Norman –

NORMAN That's why I wanted a private word with you. I've suspected it for months, but – they've been bloody clever – ingenious – led me a real paper chase – it was only the totals that put me on to it...then I started tracing back...it was off the scale...

BARRY Are we talking tens? Hundreds?

NORMAN Thousands, Barry, I'm talking thousands. You're on a sinking ship, man. If it keeps on leaking at this rate, in six months you'll be on the sea bed. Someone's been helping themselves and we're not talking petty cash or tea money. They've eaten into 50 years of accumulated capital –

BARRY But it isn't as if we haven't been monitored, is it? By your firm? Regularly. You personally lately, of course. And before that your dad for ages and ages. Since long before my time...

NORMAN *(awkwardly)* Yes, my father he – Dad – in hindsight, I think, if we're honest, he should have retired a year or two earlier than he did...in retrospect...

BARRY I can't believe it. Most of that staff have been there almost as long as I have. Totally loyal. Trustworthy. I'd stake them with my life. All of them. Sure you haven't made a mistake, Norman?

NORMAN Listen, I've got to present my report to the board by the end of this month. In view of the situation, I may need to give them some advance warning – at least the key members – the immediate family, Pauline and Debs – I don't know whether your father-in-law is...

BARRY No he's – Jess is more or less out of it these days...

NORMAN I see. Oh, dear...

BARRY Thank God, in the circumstances. This'd probably finish him.

NORMAN So it's just those two I should notify, you think? Your wife and your mother-in-law? Anyone else?

BARRY No. Oh, yes – I was forgetting. Clive. He's just joined.

NORMAN Clive?

BARRY Clive Ward. He's completely trustworthy. A solicitor. I've known him since school. He was my best man, in fact. Debs suggested he join the board. He was her idea. Listen, Norman, I do appreciate you telling me first. Giving me the heads up...

NORMAN Well, the one thing I can say about you is you're honest, Barry. I know you could never have been any part of this...

BARRY Thank you, Norman, I appreciate that.

NORMAN I mean, whoever dreamt up this little scam...well, it takes a kind of devious genius.

BARRY (*oblivious of the indirect insult*) Well, thank you, Norman. Coming from you, I appreciate that.

They shake hands. **NORMAN** *makes to leave.*

NORMAN And Barry – you will keep this tightly under wraps, won't you? Not a word to a single soul.

BARRY Not a word, Norman.

NORMAN Not till the board have been notified officially. We're talking about fraud, large scale theft, here. Certainly the police will need to be called in...

NORMAN leaves. BARRY stands for a second, still a little stunned by the news.

BARRY *(to himself)* Oh, dear! Oh, dear, oh dear!

He sits down as the lights and sound return to normal.

EZ and BARRY are still sitting on their separate benches.

EZ Hey! Sorry to interrupt. But how long do you intend keeping this up?

BARRY Sorry?

EZ All this balls about the weather? How long can you keep talking about the weather?

BARRY Well, indefinitely, really. Never gets boring does the weather, eh? Just when you've finished talking about it, it all changes. I tell you, I wouldn't want to live anywhere else but here. Nothing to talk about to strangers, otherwise, is there? No, in my opinion it's one of the things that makes this country great is the weather. *(He laughs)*

EZ *(shaking her head)* You're bloody barmy. *(She smiles one of her rare smiles)*

BARRY Ah! A smile. She's favoured us with a smile. Like the sun's suddenly come out.

EZ *(rising)* Don't raise your hopes.

BARRY Whoops! No it's gone again. Just a little gap in the clouds, there. Progress. We're getting there, as they used to say on the rail posters. I noticed they soon stopped boasting about that, though, didn't they...? Where you going?

EZ *(as she goes)* I need the toilet. Keep that warm for me, will you?

BARRY Right. *(To himself, shaking his head)* Funny girl. Got a few problems there, I wouldn't wonder.

As he sits there, the lights and background sounds change once more. It is again 2005. We are in the small yard, round the back of FOX*'s offices.*

BARRY *stands waiting.* LILY, *aged forty one, comes out to join him.*

(concerned) Alright, now?

LILY Yes, I'm OK. Better now. I just felt a bit dizzy when you told me.

BARRY It's a shock.

LILY It is. Still shaking.

BARRY Now, this mustn't go any further, Lily. That's why I wanted to tell you in private out here. We must keep this to ourselves for the time being.

LILY Oh, I will, Barry, I will. I won't tell a single soul, promise.

BARRY We must wait till the board have been notified. That'll be a day or two, yet. Then it's out of our hands, I'm afraid. They'll decide the next course of action. Which I'm afraid will certainly involve the police.

LILY Oh, dear...

BARRY Now there's nothing to worry about, Lily, as far as you're concerned. I told him, I'm standing four square behind my staff. They have been loyal to me, I intend to remain loyal to them. Trust works two ways, Lily. *(Taking her gently by the shoulders)* We stand together, eh? You and me?

He smiles at her. She suddenly bursts into tears and clings on to him.

LILY Oh, Barry...

BARRY *(startled)* What's wrong, Lily? What's the matter? *(Patting her)* There! There!

She continues to weep, holding on to him. He becomes a trifle self-conscious in such a public place.

(looking upward, nervously) Now, now, Lily, they're all watching us from the office windows...all the staff... *(Gently)* Pull yourself together, girl. It's not that bad. I've said I'll vouch for you. Come on then, lass...

LILY You're such a dear man. I'm sorry...

BARRY That's alright. Nothing to be sorry about...

LILY I'm sorry. You're such a sweet, trusting man. I'm sorry. I'm so sorry. So sorry...

She starts to move away, then stops.

(turning back) Barry...

BARRY Yes?

LILY You just take care, won't you?

BARRY Me? Why?

LILY Watch out for your wife...

BARRY Debs? What about her?

LILY Ask her where she goes every Thursday night...

BARRY Thursday? She goes to her yoga classes...

LILY Ask her, Barry. Sit her down and ask her.

LILY *goes off.*

BARRY ...she usually comes home worn out. She just needs to...lie down...for a...

Suddenly it dawns on him, what she means. He looks up at the office windows and smiles weakly at the assembled audience up there.

(calling up to them, rather ineffectually) Back to work now everybody... There's nothing to see here!

His knees give way slightly and he sits back on the bench.

(as the truth sinks in) Oh, my God!

The lights and background sounds return to normal.

As **BARRY** *sits there alone, Sequence 2 starts up with the* **SON** *standing for a moment or two with his flowers.*

BARRY *watches him, unsuspecting. The old* **MOTHER** *enters having trouble shifting her suitcase again.*

SON *(seeing her)* Mother!

MOTHER *(struggling, muttering)* My God! This is fucking ridiculous...

SON Hallo Mum. Welcome to London...

MOTHER Hallo, Horace...

BARRY *(leaping up to help her)* Hey! Let me take that for you, love. Give it here!

BARRY *grabs hold of the suitcase.*

MOTHER Thank you, mate.

BARRY Here! Horace don't just stand there. Give your old mother a hand, lad. Here let me – *(Attempting to pull it)* Bloody hell! What you got in here, love? Breeze blocks?

QUENTIN *(off, angrily)* Stop that at once please!

Startled, they all freeze. **QUENTIN** *enters indignantly.*

What the hell's going on here? This is part of a military operation. I won't have civilians interfering, getting in the firing line. Kindly stand aside, please!

BARRY Oh, I beg your pardon. I see, that was part of the...? Oh I see. *(To them both)* Very good. Very convincing.

SON Thank you!

MOTHER Thank you, sir!

QUENTIN It wasn't very good. It was appalling. Which is why we keep having to do it over and over again, Merrivale. Now carry on!

SON *(presenting her with the flowers)* Here you are, Mum, welcome to London.

MOTHER Thank you, Son.

SON *(pulling the case with difficulty)* Oh, you haven't lugged this all the way from John O'Groats, have you, Mum?

MOTHER Every foot of the way, Son.

BARRY *(as they go)* Excuse me! My advice is to make that suitcase a bit lighter in future. More realistic. Just a thought, mind...

They both exit as before, the **SON** *lugging off the impossibly heavy case.* **QUENTIN** *follows them.*

QUENTIN *(sharply, as he goes)* Keep well clear in future please. This is a carefully orchestrated military operation.

BARRY *(chastened)* Yes, I do beg your pardon. Oh, dear, my mistake...

As he sits there, the lights and sounds change again.

2011. A public park near a lake. **BARRY,** *now aged 54, is meeting up with his daughter,* **DAISY,** *now aged 26. They have not seen each other in a long time.* **DAISY** *enters and approaches him.*

DAISY *(tentatively)* Dad?

BARRY *(rising, delighted)* Daisy!

DAISY Hallo, Dad.

Uncertain how to greet each other, they make to shake hands, decide this is too formal, so rather awkwardly kiss each others' cheek.

BARRY *(studying her)* Well.

DAISY *(studying him)* Well.

Pause.

BARRY You're looking good. All grown up, eh...?

DAISY So are you.

BARRY Me? All grown older, me...

DAISY Not that old, Dad.

BARRY Well, this is nice. I'd given up hope of seeing you. Practically. With all this...

DAISY Well...

BARRY Letters. And the e-mails, of course. But they're never quite the same thing, are they?

DAISY No, well I don't get up that way very much these days. What with college – and so on. Been to see Mum a couple of times...

BARRY Her and Clive.

DAISY Do you see much of them?

BARRY Not a lot. There's still a bit of feeling there, I'm afraid...

DAISY Between you and Clive?

BARRY No, between me and your mother, really. Clive and me, we're sorted. More or less. I mean, I felt your mother rather let me down a bit, Daisy. In my time of need. I felt a little bit betrayed, you know.

DAISY Yes, I'm sure. Still, if we're honest, it was two sided, wasn't it?

BARRY Two sided? How do you mean, two sided?

DAISY Well, you and Lily.

BARRY Lily? There was nothing between me and Lily.

DAISY Nothing?

BARRY Nothing at all. We were good friends but...no.

DAISY That's not what everyone else thought...

BARRY Lily and I, we shared a few meals together...working lunches...

DAISY Every day is what I heard.

BARRY No. Not every day. *(Slight pause)* Most days, probably. I'm not denying it, we were close, certainly we were close. We were running the business together...

DAISY Which she was robbing blind.

BARRY Yes, well I – I've said I knew nothing of that, Daisy. Never even suspected. I was stunned. After all, she was your mum's maid of honour...

DAISY *(dryly)* What with Clive as your best man – you certainly knew how to pick them, you two –

BARRY ...I knew nothing about Lily at all. You must believe that...

DAISY Yes, I do. Now. I didn't at the time. Nobody did. Including the police. Tipping her off they were on to her... Letting her get clean away with most of our money. Grandad's money.

BARRY I was fully absolved, Daisy. Months, they kept on questioning me...till they finally...

DAISY They finally came to the conclusion that you were either a criminal genius or a gullible idiot, Dad. That you were led on by a more forceful personality. That's what the judge said. Lily? A more forceful personality? What the hell did that make you, Dad?

BARRY Fair enough. I owned up to being an idiot, I held my hand up to that. But I'm not an adulterer, Daisy, nor am I a criminal mastermind.

DAISY Almost prefer if you were...

BARRY What did you say?

DAISY Preferable. For me, anyway. More glamorous than local village idiot's daughter...

BARRY Glamorous? What, deceiving your mother with another woman? Stealing from my own father-in-law? <u>Glamorous?</u>

DAISY It's not what you've done or haven't done, Dad. It's what other people believe you've done, isn't it? It's how they see you.

BARRY Is that what they're teaching you with your – what you call it – your philosophical degree – is that what they're teaching you, then?

DAISY *(irritably)* Philosophy and media studies. Get that right, at least –

BARRY Is that what they're teaching you?

DAISY No, Dad, it's what life's taught me.

BARRY Well, that's bollocks, lass. Load of bollocks. I'll tell you what life's taught me. It's taught me if you start out always thinking the best of people, just occasionally maybe you'll be disappointed; but if you start out thinking the worst of everyone, chances are you'll be permanently miserable all of your life and serve you bloody right.

Slight pause.

Sorry. Just don't get cynical, Daisy. It's very smart and, how do they say, cool. But cynicism, eventually it destroys you. Sucks all the goodness out of you, lass. In time.

Silence.

Anyroad, sorry, I'm not here to lecture you. What you want to see me about? You called the meeting, didn't you? What did you want to tell me?

DAISY I'm getting married.

BARRY *(stunned but recovering quickly)* Oh. That's – that's wonderful news, love. Isn't it? I'm so happy for you. Who's the lucky bloke? When's it going to be? You're going to have it up North, aren't you? Or down here. Better up North, you know. Tell me all about him. Where d'you both meet? You must be so excited, love. Aren't you excited? You must be! *(Studying her)* You don't look very excited, I must say.

DAISY Next month and it's to be a quiet ceremony down here, just a few guests. Friends. Mark's an estate agent. He's a little bit older than me. Been married once before. He's divorced. And yes, I'm very excited... *(She hesitates)*

BARRY But.

DAISY What?

BARRY There's a but, isn't there? I can tell from your voice – same as your mother's – there's a 'but' hovering there, isn't there? But...

DAISY But I'd rather you didn't come, Dad.

Silence.

BARRY *(stunned)* Me? You don't want me there? Who's going to give you away? Clive? You haven't asked Clive to give you away, have you?

DAISY No, don't worry, I haven't asked Clive, either.

BARRY Just your Mum? Is she going to be there all on her own?

DAISY No, I haven't asked Mum either. I haven't asked any of you. I've said, just friends. Mark doesn't want his parents either. They're scarcely talking to each other.

BARRY Oh, I see. It'll just be your friends, then?

DAISY One or two. I wanted to say it to you in person, Dad. You know, not in an email. I hope you understand. It'd just be embarrassing, wouldn't it? For me it would. For both of us. If all of you came. You and Mum and Clive. Bit like a war zone.

BARRY I wouldn't want to embarrass you, lass. Quite understand.

DAISY *(kissing him)* Thank you. *(Slight pause)* Well, I must dash. I'm collecting Mark. We must all meet up sometime, mustn't we? When it's all over. Quietly. Just us three. You'd both get on. I'm sure you would.

BARRY Yes. You never know. Maybe he can find me somewhere nicer to live than where I'm currently.

DAISY Yes. Sure he could. Anyway. Bye.

BARRY Bye. *(Calling after her)* Daisy! I still love you very much you know, Michaelmas...

DAISY *(rather sadly)* Yes...

> **DAISY** *leaves. After a moment,* **BARRY** *sits again, still digesting the situation.*
>
> *As this happens, the lights and background sounds return to normal.*
>
> **EZ** *returns.*

BARRY You right, then?

EZ Yes.

BARRY I missed you. You and your cheerful chatter. Still, when you've got to go, you've got to go, eh?

EZ *(smiling faintly)* I do. Specially these days, in my case. I've missed you, too. Afraid I'd missed out on the latest weather report.

EZ *smiles.* **BARRY**'s *good humour is beginning to get to her.*

BARRY Aha! Another smile, that's two! Are we going for the record? Careful, lass, at this rate you'll be having hysterics by the time the train arrives.

EZ *(smiling)* You're barking mad. Are they all like that, where you come from?

BARRY Oh, no. In Yorkshire, I'm regarded as perfectly normal. Bit on the retiring side, even...

EZ Remind me to keep clear of that place.

BARRY Why? Frightened it might cheer you up, are you? That you'll have a good time? Go on, lass, you only live once, you know. We pass this way but once, then we're gone. Never to return...

EZ *(dryly)* Oh, that's very deep, that is...

QUENTIN *(approaching, off)* Alright, alright everyone, listen up!

BARRY Hallo, he's back.

QUENTIN *appears.*

QUENTIN Attention, people. Our train is apparently running on time –

BARRY *(winking at* **EZ***)* Miraculously, eh?

EZ *smiles again.* **BARRY** *has really got her going and knows he has.*

QUENTIN *(with a sharp look at him)* – and is due to arrive here, re-routed to this platform in precisely five and a half minutes. As far as we know, our target, Cerastes, is still aboard. He has not been sighted disembarking at any of the intermediate stations. So we're on course. You will observe that we now have four high visibility police officers positioned at the main exit there, scrutinising every disembarking passenger. In a sense they're acting as our sheepdogs.

BARRY *(winking at* EZ*)* Sheepdogs? Now, who's barking mad, eh...

EZ *giggles.* QUENTIN *glares.*

QUENTIN Hopefully, our chap will take note of them and then try and make a detour round this way to avoid them, ducking under the barrier there, which will channel him in our direction. That's the plan. The moment that happens, he's so much dead meat.

BARRY Pork pie, preferably... Do with one now, I could.

EZ *is now giggling uncontrollably, trying almost agonisingly to contain her laughter and wiping her eyes.* BARRY *continues to delight in the effect he is having on her.*

QUENTIN Now, I cannot emphasise enough that we need to take this chap alive. He's no earthly use to us dead. Alright? So positively no shooting. Clear? Now the second before that train hits the buffers...

BARRY I sincerely hope it doesn't...

EZ *continues to giggle.*

QUENTIN *(now continuously aware of them)* ...the second before it hits them, on my whistle, let's get this show rolling and on the road! On your toes, overture and beginners, stay sharp and best of luck, people!

BARRY *and* EZ *are both now sharing fits of uncontrollable giggles.*

(glaring at them) What are you two whispering and sniggering about?

EZ Sir.

BARRY Nothing.

QUENTIN Why are you both still sitting on opposite sides? I've told you it's not convincing.

BARRY We're strangers.

QUENTIN Strangers?

BARRY We thought it were more convincing, like, if we were to be strangers. We'll be discovered discussing the weather, we've got it all worked out, haven't we, Swain?

QUENTIN Convincing? Two people sat twenty feet apart, shouting to each other about the weather?

BARRY Oh, you'd be surprised. We'll give him a taster, shall we, Swain? *(Launching into his routine)* Weather's better down here than it was in Yorkshire. It were raining when I left home first thing...

> **QUENTIN** *goes off, shaking his head in disbelief.*

(continuing unabated) ...for a country the size of ours it's unbelievable how the weather can vary from place to place...

> *They are both reduced to helpless laughter.*

QUENTIN *(offstage)* Alright everyone! Stand by!

BARRY Hey! I say, I say! Swain! I've a feeling things are hotting up.

EZ *(coming back to earth)* Oh. Yes.

BARRY Listen, you can hear the train. Exciting, eh?

EZ Very.

BARRY Hope I'll recognise him. You know, come to think of it, I'm not sure now whether that moustache and glasses of his were genuine, you know.

QUENTIN *(offstage)* Stand by, everyone!

BARRY Oh, that's it! We're off. Come on, Swain, off we go then...

> **QUENTIN** *enters with his chauffeur's sign, blowing his whistle and immediately the sequences simultaneously*

get underway as before including **BARRY** *and* **EZ***'s improvisation.*

(amidst all this, launching into their routine) I say excuse me, I don't know you at all, but do you know something? The weather's a lot better down here, than it is up there... Come on, join in, Swain... It were raining in Yorkshire when I left home first thing, this morning. Did you know that?

EZ *(joining in despite herself)* You don't say?

BARRY Amazing, isn't it. You know, for such a small country as ours it's astounding how the weather can change, isn't it?

EZ Mind blowing.

BARRY Over quite small areas, too...

EZ Tiny...

BARRY I mean I can be in West Yorkshire, you know, standing in brilliant sunshine –

EZ Oh, you're from Yorkshire, then?

BARRY How did you guess? Where are you from, lass?

EZ Scotland...

BARRY Scotland? Really? I'd never have guessed that from hearing you...

EZ No, I've been south for a few years. Lost my accent...

BARRY What part of Scotland?

EZ Galashiels.

BARRY Galashiels? Now, remind me again, lass, what part of Scotland is that exactly?

EZ I haven't the faintest bloody idea...

During this the **SUSPECT**, *dressed in a distinctive red and white anorak, enters. He hesitates, seeking a way through the throng.*

QUENTIN *(excitedly)* That's him! Stop him! That's our man!

HUSBAND Here mate, catch!

He throws the baby to the SUSPECT *who involuntarily reaches out and catches it. In the effort of catching it, he trips over his feet, falling flat on his face, clutching the baby like a rugby ball.*

The others members of the team enter from all directions and gather round the SUSPECT, *producing weapons and shouting cacophonously.* EZ *throws herself across* BARRY, *protectively pinning him to the bench.*

ALL *(variously)* Keep down! On your face! Don't move! Hands behind your head! Stay there! etc. etc.

QUENTIN *(punching the air triumphantly)* Got him! Got the bastard! Got him! Alright, on your feet, you! On your feet!

The SUSPECT *is handcuffed with a plastic tie and manhandled to his feet by many hands.*

SUSPECT *(in bewilderment)* Bloody hell!

BARRY *(to* EZ*)* That's not him, you know.

QUENTIN *(not hearing this amidst the hubbub)* Right! Take him into the office there. Just till the van arrives. Take him away.

BARRY I say, excuse me, but that's definitely not him.

The SUSPECT *is bundled away by the whole team,* QUENTIN *triumphantly bringing up the rear.*

QUENTIN *(to them both)* Thanks very much, you two. You can both stand down now.

BARRY That certainly wasn't him.

QUENTIN *(ignoring him)* Like clockwork. Not a single shot fired, textbook operation.

EZ Sir!

QUENTIN Yes?

EZ Witness says that wasn't him, sir.

QUENTIN How do you mean, wasn't him?

BARRY I'm saying that wasn't the man. That wasn't the man I had the altercation with.

QUENTIN It wasn't?

BARRY No.

QUENTIN You certain?

BARRY Positive.

QUENTIN I see. *(He reflects)* No, no! Look at his behaviour, that's the behaviour of a guilty man. Running like a scared rabbit. Guilty as hell. Your chap was obviously someone different. That's it. Stand down now. I'll arrange transport to see you back home safely – er – Barry.

   QUENTIN *goes out.*

BARRY As long as it's not another helicopter, I couldn't face that again. Well. That's a bit of an anti-climax, isn't it? I'm sure it wasn't the same bloke but I expect they know best, don't they? They're the experts, after all. *(Extending his hand to* EZ*)* It's been good meeting you, Swain. A pleasure spending time with you. I can't say I've got to know you very well, lass, but still. Then again you didn't get to know me very well, either, did you? Another time, eh? Perhaps we'll meet again sometime? Who knows? Probably not, but... Anyroad, I got two smiles out of you, at least, eh? That's something, isn't it?

EZ It's been good to meet you, Barry. You know what? You've gone some way to restoring my faith, mate.

BARRY How do you mean?

EZ My faith in people.

BARRY That's nice. It's nice when that happens, isn't it? *(He smiles)*

EZ *(smiling back)* Yes. Nice.

BARRY Hey! Three! That's the world record. Three smiles! I've done it!

He dances round a little. EZ stands watching him, smiling.

(triumphantly) Champion! Yes! Yes! Yes!

QUENTIN *appears in the doorway. They stop.*

QUENTIN As you were. That wasn't him. Wrong man. Wrong man, altogether.

BARRY Ah. *(Slight pause)* Told you so, didn't I?

EZ Who is he, then?

QUENTIN Some wretched student travelling without a ticket.

EZ Bet he won't try that again.

QUENTIN Could have been worse, anyway. We could have accidentally shot him. Fortunate for him we needed Cerastes alive.

EZ Unfortunate for him he happened to be wearing a distinctive red and white anorak?

QUENTIN No, not a coincidence. This student was apparently sitting across from a chap who was wearing one, who took it off during the journey, and left it behind on his seat when he got off again. So this student waited for a minute or two, then promptly helped himself to it.

BARRY Students aren't what they used to be, are they?

EZ Where did this bloke get off?

QUENTIN *(grimly)* Stevenage.

EZ *(sardonically)* And slipped through the ring of steel?

QUENTIN Yes. Apparently. (*Looking to change the subject*) Barry, regarding your journey home. Transport were wondering whether you'd prefer to take your trip home by rail? Rather than risking another helicopter trip? I mean, it's entirely up to you...

BARRY Oh, I'd much prefer the train, thank you...

QUENTIN First class of course...

BARRY No, no, there's no need for that. I can travel standard, I'm used to standard –

QUENTIN No, no. It's all included...

BARRY I prefer standard, if you don't mind. You tend to meet more interesting people in standard.

QUENTIN (*doubtfully*) Yes?

BARRY I mean, you never get the chance for a decent chat in first class, do you? I've seen them there, whenever I've passed through, sitting in silence in their suits, scowling at their screens and texting. They all seem a bit grumpy, if you ask me. I prefer to be amongst real people. Kiddies and all. Put up with them. If you don't mind?

QUENTIN (*rather mystified*) Yes, just as you like. Well, I'll go and arrange the ticket. Standard? You're sure?

BARRY If it's no trouble.

QUENTIN *goes off.* **EZ** *belches.*

EZ Pardon.

BARRY Better out than in.

EZ *starts to rummage in her stuff.*

Well. What's next for you. Back to the barracks, are you?

EZ No.

BARRY Ah.

EZ Excuse me, I need to take one of these...

He wanders away from her a little. EZ *is searching for her pills, back in her thoughts again.* BARRY *stops as he sees someone approaching along the platform.*

BARRY *(half to himself)* Hallo... That's odd. *(Straining his eyes, quietly)* It could be...if I'm not very much mistaken...

EZ *(still preoccupied with her rucksack, amused)* What's he on about now?

BARRY *(still quietly, half to himself)* ...yes. It is. It's him! Good gracious. That's crafty. The crafty so and so...

EZ continues to ignore him, smiling and shaking her head, well used to him chuntering on by now.

CERASTES enters. He is dressed as a train guard, apparently coming off duty from the recently arrived train. He walks casually as if in no particular hurry. BARRY *intercepts him.*

I say, excuse me...

CERASTES Yes, sir. How can I help you?

EZ glances up but then continues searching in her luggage for her pills.

BARRY Well, for a kick off you can help me by settling your outstanding PCN.

CERASTES Sorry?

BARRY *(smiling)* Your parking ticket. In Harrogate the other day. You can't have forgotten me, surely.

CERASTES *(smiling)* Oh, yeah... Mr Traffic Warden, of course.

BARRY *(smiling)* Yes, me. The bloke you nearly ran over...

EZ is suddenly taking notice but cannot quite believe what she is witnessing.

CERASTES *(smiling)* Get out of my way, you clown, or I'll run you over again...

BARRY *(very pleasantly, smiling)* Insults and threats, I'm afraid will get you precisely nowhere. I'm sorry, but you were guilty of an infringement of parking regulations and I'm afraid you have therefore been formally issued with a PCN, a Penalty Charge Notice, payable by cheque or postal order or in certain cases online...

CERASTES Alright! Alright! *(Reaching into his jacket)* You want me to pay, I'll pay, you officious little bastard...

EZ *looks up, far too late.*

BARRY Well, not here and now, no... I'm not entitled personally –

EZ *(realising the danger, shouting)* Barry! Be careful!

BARRY – to collect formal payment of a PCN. Your best course is to – Ooooh!

CERASTES *appears to have punched* **BARRY** *in the abdomen, swiftly and efficiently. In fact, as we see when he withdraws his hand he has in fact stabbed him.* **CERASTES** *leaves* **BARRY** *standing, more startled than hurt initially, and walks away, wiping the knife on the sleeve of his uniform. He walks casually away from* EZ, *who is momentarily frozen. He exits, still apparently in no hurry.*

EZ *(recovering)* Hey, you! Hold it right there! Hold it there, you!

She scrabbles in her bag again and produces a service revolver.

(yelling after **CERASTES***)* Stop! Stop or I'll shoot. I said stop! This is your last warning! Stop!

She holds the gun steady and fires. She stares after her quarry for a second. Then stands, momentarily shaken by her action, still holding the gun.

QUENTIN, *alarmed by the sound, enters.* WISBY *also arrives behind him, gun in hand.*

QUENTIN What the hell are you playing at, Swain? Put down that gun, at once!

EZ *(dazed)* What?

WISBY *(excitedly)* Put down the gun! Put down the gun! Lay the gun on the floor!

QUENTIN You've just shot a railway official, woman! I hope you realise that!

QUENTIN *hurries off past* BARRY *after* CERASTES.

WISBY Put down the gun, at once!

EZ, *recovering, puts the gun on the ground.* BARRY *meanwhile, ignored by the others, is beginning to feel the pain.*

BARRY *(clutching his midriff)* Oh! Oh! Oh!

He staggers slightly, still uncertain as to what has exactly happened to him. He withdraws his hand and seems surprised to see it is covered in blood.

Oh!

EZ *(moving to him, alarmed)* Barry?

WISBY *(circling her, pointing his gun and yelling)* Don't move! Hands in the air! Do you hear? Flat on your face on the ground! This is your last warning!

EZ *takes* BARRY's *arm and steadies him.*

EZ Barry, are you alright, mate?

WISBY This is absolutely your final warning! If you do not get down on the ground, hands behind your head, I shall fire. You have been warned!

EZ *(angrily)* Oh, piss off, will you? Can't you see this man's hurt?

WISBY, *rather bemused at this response, lowers his gun.*

(sharply, in her best parade ground manner) And call an ambulance, quickly, soldier! On the double!

WISBY *(by reflex, confused)* Sir! Ma'am! Sir!

He backs off and exits.

EZ *leads* BARRY *gently to a bench.*

EZ Sit down, sit down here. Let's take a look at you.

BARRY I think he must have stabbed me, you know. With a knife. It happened so quick, I didn't realise... It felt more like he'd punched me...

EZ *(seating him)* Alright. Sit down here.

She starts to undo his clothing, in an attempt to see the extent of the damage.

BARRY *(as she does this)* I didn't realise. I thought he was maybe going for his cheque book, you know, or maybe his credit cards...ooh it's beginning to hurt a bit now. Is it bad? Can you see how bad it is, lass?

EZ Yes, it's pretty bad...ambulance is coming, Barry...don't worry...ambulance is on its way...

BARRY Thank goodness for that. Think I'm going to need one, you know. *(Another spasm of pain)* Oh, dear! Oh dear, oh dear! No, you see, if he had been reaching for his credit cards or his cheque book, then I had to tell him, we're not authorised, you see...

EZ Barry, save your energy. Try not to talk too much, mate... Try not to talk? – Jesus, what am I saying, asking you not to talk?

BARRY *(panting slightly)* Oh, it's getting calmer, now...things are a bit misty like...but calmer!

EZ Won't be long, Barry. Try to breathe. Breathe normally...

QUENTIN *enters angrily.*

Where's that ambulance?

QUENTIN Well, we got our man. We successfully cornered Cerastes. And now thanks to you, Swain, he's stone bloody dead, isn't he? Worse than useless to us now.

EZ Where's the ambulance? I asked for an ambulance?

QUENTIN No point in calling an ambulance now, Swain. Didn't you hear me? He's dead! You shot the man dead!

EZ *(angrily)* Not for him! For this man, you stupid arsehole!

QUENTIN *(shaken, quietly)* This is all going down on your record, Swain. Obscene language to a senior officer, failure to obey orders and improper use of an illegal firearm.

BARRY *groans.*

EZ Alright, Barry? Stay with us, mate. It's on its way.

QUENTIN How is he?

EZ *looks at him.*

(the final straw) Oh, my God! What a day...disaster. Utter disaster!

QUENTIN *goes out.*

EZ *(gently)* Barry! Barry! Are you still with us? Barry?

BARRY *(woozily)* Who's that? Is that you, Daisy, love?

EZ *(kneeling by him)* No, it's me Barry. It's Ez. Swain.

BARRY *(slightly delirious)* Swain? Daisy Swain... Daisy chain... Michaelmas Daisy. *(Stroking her hair)* Glad you came, love.

EZ No, I'm not... Barry it's Ez...it's Swain...

BARRY Your Dad's not feeling so good at the moment, Daisy, darling...

EZ No... Oh. *(She gives up trying to make him understand)*

BARRY ...but you must be a good girl, look after your mum, Daisy. Promise me you'll do that, love...promise me...you must promise me...

EZ Yes, I promise...

BARRY Promise your Dad now, darling?

EZ I promise, Dad...

BARRY That's a good girl. I love you so much, Daisy. You know that?

EZ I know that Dad. I love you too...

BARRY More than anything in the world, Daisy...

EZ More than anything in the world, Dad...

They both remain there. **BARRY**, *now very weak,* **EZ** *kneeling beside him, allowing him to continue gently stroking her hair.*

She starts to cry softly, which is probably the first time this restrained young woman, who till now has kept her feelings so proudly in check, has allowed herself to cry in a long while.

The lights and the backgrounds subtly alter as two paramedics enter with a gurney. The medics gently lift **EZ** *away from* **BARRY**. *After a brief examination, they gently move him on to the trolley.*

As this happens, the two children, **YOUNG ESMÉ** *and* **YOUNG DAISY** *appear from separate directions, move slowly together and, holding each other's hand, silently watch the proceedings from a distance.*

The gurney is slowly wheeled off with **EZ** *in close attendance.*

The lights fade to the children who finally separate, turn and leave in different directions, returning to their respective and special places in **EZ** *and* **BARRY**'s *memories. The lights fade to: –*

Blackout.

End of Play

PROPS

ACT ONE
Disused platform at a London mainline railway station
Two or three empty benches
Chauffeur's hat
Hand-written Chauffeur's sign, "GROOMBRIDGE CHEMICALS"
Folded baby stroller with bedding
Baby
Bunch of flowers
Heavy suitcase on wheels
Three paper mugs with hot coffee
Personal stereo x2
Heavy rucksack
Map
Whistle
Mobile phone
EZ's documentation
Small suitcase
Plastic bottles of coke and straws
Stopwatch
EZ's rucksack
Holdall
Two overnight bags
Weapons
Plastic tie for handcuffs

ACT TWO
Toolbox
Envelope of money
Train tickets
Bags and luggage
Knife
Service Revolver (EZ)
WISBY's gun
Gurney

LIGHTING

ACT ONE
Lights change (p12)
Lights change (p14)
Lights change (p17)
Lights change (p22)
Lights return to normal (p24)
Lights return to normal (p29)
Lights change again (p32)
Lights change once more (p33)
Lights return to normal (p35)
Lights return to normal (p38
The lights change again (p39)
Lights change (p42)
Lights change again (p43)
Lights cross-fade to normality (p46)
Lights change again to another station platform (p49)
The lights return to normal (p53)
Blackout (p57)

ACT TWO
Lights change (p64)
Lights return to normal (p67)
Lights change (p68)
Lights return to normal (p69)
Lights change again (p70)
Lights change as we return to normal (p71)
Lights change again (p72)
Lights return to normal (p75)
The lights change again to a corridor (p77)
Lights return to normal (p78)
Lights change again - sunshine (p79)
Lights return to normal (p81)
Lights change again (p82)
Lights return to normal (p84)
Lights change again (p86)
Lights return to normal (p91)
Lights subtly alter (p104)

Lights fade (p105)
Blackout (p105)

SOUND EFFECTS

ACT ONE
Distant sounds of the station going about its normal business (p1)
Quartet of football supporters starts to sing drunkenly (p2)
Offstage groan from football supporters (p6)
Footballers start up their song again (p7)
A chorus of protest from off (p10)
Background sounds change slightly (p12)
A distant triumphal military band is heard (p12)
Background sounds change (band music) (p14)
Faint sounds of planes and birdsong (p17)
Solemn music is heard distantly (p17)
The sound changes (p17)
Sound change (p22)
Sound of a bus departing (p22)
Sounds return to normal (p24)
Cheering from the direction of the football supporters (p26)
Some boo-ing from the football supporters (p26)
Background sounds return to normal (p29)
Sounds change once more (p33)
Background sounds return to normal (p35)
Background sounds change again (p39)
Sounds change again (p42)
An approaching train is heard (p53)

ACT TWO
Some cheering from the direction of the football supporters (p63)
Some boo-ing from the football supporters (p63)
Sounds change again (p64)
Sounds return to normal (p67)
Background sounds change (p68)
Sound returns to normal (p69)
Background sounds change again (p70)

Background sounds as we return to normal (p71)
Background sounds change again (p72)
Sound return to normal (p75)
Sound change again (p78)
Distant passing traffic (p79)
Sound return to normal (p81)
Sound change again (p82)
Sounds return to normal (p84)
Sounds change again (p86)
Sound change again (p91)
Gun is fired (p101)
Backgrounds sounds subtly alter (p104)

VISIT THE SAMUEL FRENCH BOOKSHOP AT THE ROYAL COURT THEATRE

Browse plays and theatre books, get expert advice and enjoy a coffee

Samuel French Bookshop
Royal Court Theatre
Sloane Square
London
SW1W 8AS
020 7565 5024

Shop from thousands of titles on our website

 samuelfrench.co.uk

 samuelfrenchltd

 samuel french uk

Lightning Source UK Ltd.
Milton Keynes UK
UKHW010847010219
336564UK00006B/653/P